Still in Hollywood

Still in Hollywood

Darrin Atkins

Writers Club Press
San Jose New York Lincoln Shanghai

Still in Hollywood

Writers Club Press
an imprint of iUniverse.com, Inc.

For information address:
iUniverse.com, Inc.
5220 S 16th, Ste. 200
Lincoln, NE 68512
www.iuniverse.com

ISBN: 0-595-19063-4

Printed in the United States of America

Contents

Prologue

I'm going back. Yes, I'm going back to Hollywood and Los Angeles and I don't know why the hell I ever left and if you've ever lived there then you know what I mean, you know that some people just love the damn city terribly and can't get over it at all and want to go back as soon as they can. Sure, it's crowded and there's horrible traffic down there but man oh man it is so wonderful at times with the perfect, sunny, glorious beaches, the long, breathtaking boulevards, the passionate concerts, the unending stretches of palm trees, the snow-capped mountains in the distance, the sunny, happy mornings, the constant buzz of activity, the irrepressible personalities, and the eternal hope of the aspiring actors and singers. All in all, it's simply irresistible, to me it really is.

I'm going back next week. I've lived there twice before so I know what I'm in for and how to get around and what I need to do in order to survive. Things will be better this time. I won't have much money but I'm not going to need it. See, I'm going to camp up in the mountains in the national forests that tower over the metropolis, and when I want to I'll call to see if there's work available and if there is then I'll just drive right over to the movie studios and wait until someone says lights, camera, action and I'll do what they tell me to do and be patient and work hard and my hard work will take me far, at least I hope so.

I'm going back and I can't wait. The last time I lived in Los Angeles I had a wonderful and interesting time and fell in love with this Japanese girl, yes the one on the cover of this book, and we did all kinds of different things and a lot happened between us and I'll get to all that shortly, I will indeed, and you'll see and you'll be moved by it all, by how this is a true story, an autobiographical, non-fiction one in its truest form. And I'll even tell you about the first time I lived in Los Angeles, when I worked at this movie magazine and lived in Beverly Hills and how all these other things happened that set things in motion for the second time for me there and even for this time now, soon so very soon, when I move there again for one last attempt, one last try, one last big, big effort.

Just remember that I'm going back, I'm going back real soon, I stayed away too long, it's time for me to return, I'm going back to L.A., I can't wait for the days to pass, I have a deep longing to return, I miss so much about it, and this time I'm not going to leave, no I'm not and you best believe what I say, how I won't go away. I'm going to stay there until I make it big and I don't care what I have to do. I'm going back and I'm going to make it this time and pretty soon I'll be a household name and you'll read all about me in the papers. Just wait and see. I always do what I say I'm going to do. I'm going back. I'm going back right now. This very second. I'm going back in more ways than one. On the eve of my departure, I'm going back in time as I recall what used to be, what happened way back when, how the ball got rolling, how I wasn't even out of Reno yet when everything began. I'm going back, indeed I am. I'm going back, yes sir, yes ma'am. I'm going back right now.

PART 1

Premiere Magazine

I

Premiere magazine. It was by far and away my favorite publication and I wanted to work there desperately. It was late 1994 and I was living in Reno and nearing the end of an internship at Nevada magazine and I was also working at the Reno Gazette-Journal, though not in any sort of glamorous position in the editorial or art departments, no nothing like that at all, unfortunately. Just some simple position of a sub-division of the circulation department.

I wanted to move out of Nevada and was prepared to do so and all I needed was an opportunity somewhere else. I didn't care how different or difficult a new city would be. All I cared about was that I would be out of Reno and away from my life there. I had grown sick and weary of my existence in Nevada and I missed California where I had gotten spoiled by the unending options for recreation and entertainment and adventure.

So one day, having realized that I wanted to work at Premiere magazine above and beyond any other place, I designed a resume and cover letter and sent them along with a copy of the magazine where I was working, the state tourist magazine, to the intern coordinator at Premiere. It was early November and I knew it would be perfect for me if I could get an internship beginning some time in the early part of the coming year. I could not bear the thought of another year in Reno and the thought of starting 1995 in Los Angeles appealed to me greatly, especially at a magazine that covered the entertainment industry. Oh, that sounded grand, indeed it did, so very grand. And so I waited for a response.

Two weeks later I received a call from the internship coordinator at Premiere and she wanted to schedule me for an interview in early December, that is if I was still interested in the internship. Of course I was and so I scheduled it for a day when I was off from work, on a Friday in fact, and that was fine with her.

I couldn't believe it. I tried to remain calm because an interview didn't necessarily always result in a job offer, but an interview was a huge step and I could feel things starting to change for me for the better. I just knew that I would do well during the interview and that I would be hired and that it would be the greatest thing ever and I would remember the internship for the rest of my life. I could feel it deep down inside me. It was my destiny and my destiny was me.

A week passed and then I had to buy the plane ticket in order to get a good price on it. I had no money to speak of and so I had to borrow what I could from my girlfriend at the time and I just hate doing that, hate borrowing money because it's so hard to do, because it means that I don't have enough. But I got my ticket and then the day came, that Friday morning, and I got a ride to the airport and boarded the plane and it was weird to leave because I knew I would be back that same evening.

I landed at the LAX airport and knew where I had to go next, where the building was located where I was going to have my interview, because I had located it on a map of L.A. I had plenty of time to get there because I had arrived so early in the day and my interview wasn't until one o'clock. The building was located in Santa Monica and I felt grateful that the airport wasn't too far from that city. I walked around the airport terminal and then followed the signs to the escalators which led downstairs and to the buses. I found the airport shuttle bus and stepped up to talk to the driver.

"I'm looking for a bus that'll take me to Santa Monica," I said.

"Hop on."

"It's this bus?" I asked, surprised.

"No, but I can take you to the bus stop where you can get on the right one."

"Oh, I see. How much for this one here?" I dug into my pocket for some change.

"It's free, provided by the airport."

"Great."

I sat down and waited and soon the bus was on its way. It only took a few minutes for the bus to get to the central bus stop. I got out when we got there and I headed over to some big bus route signs. I looked at the L.A. city map I had brought with me, which I had gotten from the auto club, and compared it to the bus route I saw in front of me. It didn't take me long to find out which bus I needed to ride. I glanced at the buses that were already there and was surprised to see the one I needed to be very close to me. I quickly made my way over to it.

"Does this bus go to Santa Monica?" I asked.

"Sure does," said the driver. "But not for another few minutes."

"Great."

I paid the fare, got on, and sat down and relaxed a bit. It was a very nice sunny day and everything was going much better and quicker than I expected. The bus departed after a bit and soon we were off and onto the busy L.A. streets. I followed both my city map and the map on the bus closely and within ten minutes we were in Santa Monica and I had to decide where to stop. I knew the bus I was on didn't go right to the building where my interview was going to be, but I didn't think it mattered because of how many hours I had before the interview. I had gotten to Santa Monica much faster than I thought I would.

Finally, I got off at a stop and looked around. I found a bench nearby and sat down. I looked at the map and realized that I was pretty close to where I needed to be. Because of how much time I had, I decided to walk around. I was close to a place called Third Street Promenade and I had never even heard about it before so I walked around there for a while and loved it instantly, loved the multitude of shops and proximity to the beach and wonderful smells that emanated form the restaurants. I could even see the beach from that area.

Then I remembered that I knew some friends who lived in Santa Monica. I found their address, located it on my map, and decided to go pay them a visit. It was about two miles from where I was and I didn't mind walking, didn't mind it at all, especially given the free time I had. It took me quite a while but finally I found their apartment and knocked on the door and I was quite tired from the long walk. Someone inside had the music turned up really loud so I knocked harder but still nothing happened. I waited a while and tried to look in the window but to no avail. Again I knocked really hard and then a young man came to the door.

"Hello?" he said.

"Hi, my name's Darrin. I'm a college friend of Lorrie's."

"Yes, come in. I'm Paul. She said you were going to be in town today." I walked in and shook his hand.

"Have a seat," he said. "Good to meet you."

"Sorry I didn't call first. I took a bus from the airport and it stopped pretty close to here."

"You came at the right time because I was just about to leave and Lorrie won't be back until tonight. She's told me a lot about you."

"There's not much to tell."

"You have an interview at Premiere? That's impressive, for this town at least."

"It's just for an internship. The pay's not so great."

"Did you bring a suit jacket?" he asked.

"No, you think I need one? I have a tie."

"Sure you do. I'll grab one out of my closet."

I waited in the living room of the apartment as Paul searched his closet. He came back after he found one and presented it to me. "See if it fits," he said. "I haven't used it in a while."

I tried it on. "It fits perfectly. Thanks a lot. I don't go to that many job interviews."

"Oh, you've gotta wear a suit jacket. Even if you're applying for a part-time internship. It shows that you care."

"You're right."

"What time is your interview and where is it?"

"It's at one o'clock in Santa Monica, near Bundy and Olympic."

"I know where that is. I've gotta do some shopping today so if you want I can take you there now."

"That's fine. I don't mind waiting there."

"All right. And then I can pick you up around two and get you back to the airport so you don't have to take the buses all around."

"Great, I really appreciate it." It was all incredibly nice of him to do this and I hadn't expected it at all.

"Don't mention it. Any friend of Lorrie's is a friend of mine."

I couldn't believe how lucky I was in actually finding Paul and Lorrie's apartment, and then to have Paul home and then him having free time to take me around town and for him to be willing to do so was just great luck on my part. It seemed too good to be true. It saved a lot of time, effort and confusion for me. Though I could have taken the bus back to the airport and I had the schedules with me, there was always the off chance that I would take the wrong one and end up in some place like downtown and be totally lost.

Within a few minutes we left and Paul drove and I looked all around at L.A. and how nice it seemed to me. "What is this area called?" I asked. "Is this Santa Monica here?"

"Actually we just left it but we'll get back into it in a minute or two. See, the actual city lines are parallel to certain streets. There's way too many small cities in L.A."

"Oh, I see, sort of."

"It takes some getting used to."

Soon we found the building for my interview and Paul dropped me off. "I'll be back on this street at two," he said. "Right here."

"I'll see you then," I said. Thanks again."

"No need to thank me."

He took off and I straightened my tie. I had my resume in a little folder in my backpack and I knew I would use it soon. I had some time so I decided to walk around the neighborhood and kill a few minutes. Pretty soon it became close to my interview time so I went into the building and looked around. I liked the suit jacket I had borrowed and I felt that it made me appear more professional.

I found the name of the magazine on a board in the lobby so I took the elevator to that floor and followed the signs all the way down the hall and looked on the right side until I found the correct number. I was very nervous and didn't know what to think or do. I opened the door and stepped inside. There was a desk to my left and a nice, attractive Asian lady was seated there.

"Hello," she said.

"Hi." I made sure the door closed behind me, then I turned back to her. "My name is Darrin Atkins. I have an interview at one o'clock."

"Okay, let me call her and let her know. You can have a seat if you want."

"Thanks."

I turned behind me and walked over and sat down on a small sofa. Then I looked around and on the walls and there were these very large, colorful, exciting movie posters. They were hung all over the place, from the area I was in and all the way down the part of the hallway that I could see. It was terribly exciting and I knew it was all about Hollywood and this place had to be the coolest place in town and I couldn't believe how lucky I was in getting just the chance of an interview here. I told myself that the experience of being here was something in and of itself and even if I didn't get the internship I would be happy and content in knowing that I made an attempt at it. I glanced at the young Asian lady and she was terribly cute and her clothes were just as professional as can be.

Soon I heard someone come down the hallway and then come over to me. I stood up.

"Are you Darrin?" she asked.

"Yes, nice to meet you."

"I'm Eliza Krause, come on back."

I grabbed my backpack and followed her and said thank you again to the Asian lady and she said that I was welcome. I walked down the long hallway and there were more and more movie posters all over the place, real big ones with huge posters in expensive frames. It was like heaven to me and I couldn't think of a cooler place in the world and it was hard to take in given all the years I had read and subscribed to Premiere and how I had always read it all from cover to cover.

We turned left at the end of the hallway and then went into her office, which was the third one on the right.

"Have a seat," she said. I sat down and tried to calm myself. "I have your resume here and the magazine you sent me with your name in it. Did you have a nice flight from Reno?"

"Oh, fine. This is actually my first time in L.A."

"Are you thinking of moving here?"

"Of course I would relocate if I got the position."

"That's good to know. Why don't you tell me about yourself?"

I explained where I was at in my life and my recent journalism experience. "I just finished an internship at Nevada magazine and my job at the Reno Gazette-Journal will be ending soon."

"Why is it ending?" she asked.

"I've been working in a special magazine section of the circulation department and they've decided to close it down so that means all of the positions will be eliminated. That's fine with me."

"But they would give you another position?"

"Oh yes, if I wanted it they would give me something. But it's my option and I can leave if I want to."

"That's nice. So I assume you like movies?"

"Oh yes."

I told her about the movies I had seen recently, some of my favorites, how I had been a long-time subscriber to the magazine, and how I had been involved in theater and drama in college and high school. And I relayed my interest in a variety of different movies, how I liked art-house films, how I cared for Bogart and Cagney films, and I communicated my preferences for certain actors and actresses.

"Do you know anybody in town here?"

"Oh yes, I have my friend who brought me here today. He lives with a female friend of mine from college. I've just up and moved to other cities before so it's no big deal for me. And my parents are very supportive and have said they would help me out this time for sure because they know how big an opportunity this is."

"We can only pay you minimum wage and only offer about twelve hours a week."

"That's fine. I can pick up other work through temp agencies and part-time jobs."

"It's expensive, living here in L.A."

"I know, but I'll manage just fine. I have a lot of confidence in my ability to start over."

Then she asked me a lot of other questions about my experience with computers and my work habits and I answered those the best that I could. She was a very nice, considerate person and I felt deep down that she liked me at least a little bit and I knew for a fact that the suit jacket was a very good idea because the interview was more formal than I thought it would be.

"All right, that's all the questions I have. Do you have any for me?"

And of course I knew I had to ask some so I asked her about the possibility of being hired full-time after the internship, I asked her about the writers, I asked her about anything I could think of just to show that I was interested in everything pertaining to the magazine, which I was. But I knew not to ask too many questions.

"That's all I can think of," I said.

"Okay, let me walk you out. Thanks so much for flying down from Reno. I'll be calling people during the early part of next week."

"Thank you."

Then she took me back to the exit and another young person was seated there and I figured she was going to be interviewed for the internship like me and I didn't feel so special after all and I wondered how I could possibly compete with all the other people who wanted to intern at Premiere. I walked down the hallway and out of the lobby of the building and went outside and sat down near the fountain. I could certainly imagine myself working for the magazine but I didn't see how I could possibly overcome all of the little things that were on my mind. As it was I had borrowed money from my girlfriend just for the plane ticket for the interview. I had virtually no savings because of how I had volunteered at a magazine in Nevada for the experience and worked part-time at the newspaper. Those were tough decisions but the right ones given my desire for a journalism or writing career.

I thought all of all this as I sat outside and waited for Paul. I waited and watched the cars that went by. I felt lucky that he was willing to pick me up and take me to the airport. After a while he showed up and I found him and walked across the street to his car.

"Sorry about the wait," he said. "I nearly forgot where I dropped you off."

"Thanks again," I said.

"No problem at all. I like driving to the airport."

We headed in that direction and I thought about my interview.

"You think you'll get it?" he asked.

"Hard to say. The lady seemed very nice and she asked me if I was willing to relocate and of course I said yes. And I talked about movies a lot and what I liked and I'm sure that didn't hurt."

"Oh, you'll get it for sure. They don't pay much I bet."

"Not at all and I said I didn't care about that. I just want it for the experience."

"You've got nothing to worry about."

Soon we arrived at the airport, at the terminal for my airline which was located at the second level of the airport along with all of the other airlines for departures. The arrival section was located on the bottom section of the airport.

"Thanks again," I said. "And please tell Lorrie that I'm sorry I missed her. I wanted so much to see her again." I took off my suit jacket and handed it back to him. And thanks for this."

"You're welcome. Good to meet you. I'll tell Lorrie about everything."

"All right, see you next year." I was confident that I would get the job.

I shut the car door and walked into the terminal with my backpack over my shoulder. Somehow everything had gone quite well and I was back at the airport early, way early than I thought possible. I went to my airline to check in. I didn't mind the fact that I'd have to wait ninety minutes before the plane left. I was simply relieved that my interview was over and I was back at the airport.

"You just got here," said the woman at the airline counter after examining my ticket. She was right, of course, because I had arrived about five hours earlier in the day. "And now you're leaving?"

"I know," I laughed. "I just came here for a job interview."

"That's funny." She gave me my ticket and I went to the waiting area for my plane. My time in L.A. and had gone really well and I just knew that I would be coming back to live there in less than a month, oh how I just knew that it was going to happen and I could only imagine what things would be like for me.

2

Soon I was back in Reno. That weekend passed and so did Monday and Tuesday morning and I started to worry that I wouldn't get the internship. During the afternoon I went to see a movie to get my mind off whether or not I would get a call from Premiere. But when I got back from the movie I noticed a message on my answering machine and it was from the woman with whom I had my interview. I quickly called her back and prayed that she was still there. Luckily she was and to my great satisfaction and relief she offered me the internship position and I gladly accepted. She told me to report for my first day of work on the third day of January and I said that I would. I thanked her very much and hung up. And I couldn't believe it because I was going to move to L.A. and would work at a movie magazine and I would be getting out of Reno for good and things would be better for me and I would have the time of my life. It was more than I would have thought possible just a month before and here I was getting all that I wanted. It was amazing and I was excited about my prospects.

I stayed in Reno for a few weeks and then packed up my things and went back home to Stockton to stay with my family for a week. I left Stockton during the last week of December and headed for L.A. I had no idea where I would stay and had just six hundred dollars with me, most of which had been loaned to me by my parents. I didn't know what I was going to do but I didn't care just so long as I was able to work at Premiere and finish the internship which was supposed to last until May. I didn't care if I had to sleep on the beach and starve.

I had a full week before I was supposed to begin work and I figured that would give me plenty of time to get settled. I knew that L.A. was quite expensive a place to live and I figured right off that I wouldn't be able to live in a normal apartment. I told myself that the worst case scenario was that I would just live out of my car if I had to, that I could sleep on the beaches in the daytime, that the weather wouldn't get so cold that I couldn't sleep outside if that's what things came to. I was just glad to be out of Reno and I certainly wasn't going to go back there. Man, no way in hell I was going back.

At around nine o'clock I hit some morning traffic in L.A. and it was just horrible and took forever to get anywhere, but that didn't bother me too much because I wasn't in a hurry and didn't have to be anywhere at any particular time. I just had to find a place for the night. And then the traffic stopped for a while, stopped right in the middle of a giant freeway, and soon ambulances came down the freeway and passed us and more time passed as all of the cars stood motionless on the freeway. I wondered if traffic was always like this in L.A. Soon, thankfully, the traffic started moving again.

I wasn't even sure where to begin looking for a place to stay. I figured the best thing for me would be to find a residence close to Premiere so it wouldn't take me too long to get there. So I made my way to Santa Monica and got off at an exit and found a grocery store and stopped there. I found some apartment listings and of course the costs were way out of my range. What I really needed was a place for the night so I perused the motel listings and found a place on a street I was familiar with, on the street on which Paul and Lorrie lived. I found the place on my map and headed there. I wanted to have a place where I could rest and stay, if only for one night, so I could get oriented to everything and have a base.

The motel was a small one with only about ten rooms and it didn't look too grand but none of that mattered. I got there and paid for that night. I felt a lot better after that, knowing that at least I had a place to stay for the evening and could stay there after that if I needed to. There was a phone in my room so I used it and called the ads for apartments in the newspaper that were very inexpensive. A lot of them were in locations I couldn't find or were too far from where I wanted to live. I felt a sense of urgency because I knew I wouldn't be able to afford the motel for too long. I called some other places but most of them had answering machines so I didn't even bother with them. Then I saw something that seemed perfect, a room that was rented on a weekly basis in Beverly Hills, a city that was fairly close to Santa Monica and only a few miles from my motel and about the same distance from Premiere. A weekly rent would be perfect because I wouldn't have to give them all my money at once. I called the number quickly.

"I'm calling about your room," I said. "Do you still have it available?"

"Yes we do, but someone's coming to look at it tonight."

"Can I come first?"

"Sure, whoever gets here first gets the place."

"Okay, I'm on my way."

I hung up, grabbed my keys and wallet, locked the door, and raced to my car. I started driving and followed the map and soon I was there and it didn't take me long at all. I parked right on the street and raced over to the complex and knocked on the office door.

"My name's Darrin," I said. "I called ten minutes ago about the room."

"That was fast. Hold on, I'll get the key."

I waited and then he took me up some stairs. "It's really small," he said.

"As long as there's a bed and a bathroom."

"There is, but not much else."

And he was right. It had those things, a very tiny kitchen area, and not much space to even move around after that. But it had what I needed.

"I can rent this by the week?" I asked.

"Yes."

"All right, I'll take it."

We went downstairs and filled out the forms and I paid for the first week, to start the following evening because I had already paid for my motel room.

"Thanks a lot," I said. "I'll be back tomorrow."

"You're welcome, see you then."

I went back to my car and was greatly disappointed to see a parking ticket on it, but I felt so great about getting the room that I hardly cared at all. I felt a hell of a lot better. I went back to my motel room in Santa Monica and relaxed and felt relieved because I had found a permanent apartment for myself. In the evening I walked up and down the street and was enchanted by the palm trees and the beautiful sky and the cool, comfortable ocean breeze. I was happy now and knew that the most difficult part of my move to L.A. was over and the next day I would move into my apartment in Beverly Hills. It seemed unreal.

3

Then Monday came and it was time for me to start my internship at Premiere, the movie magazine. It was a rainy day so I made sure to leave early so I would get there on time. The last thing I wanted was to be late on my first day of work. But on the way I remembered the parking situation near the building and I figured I might need some money. So I decided to stop at an ATM machine along the way and then I couldn't find one and got lost and it got closer and closer to the time when I was supposed to start work. So I just gave up on the whole money thing and decided to get to work and take my chances. But luckily, close to work, I found a bank and an ATM and got some money and made it to work right on time.

I hurried up to the third floor and turned right and went down the hallway and stopped right at the door. I was very excited about my new job and didn't care one bit that the wages were insignificant and that I was only going to be scheduled for a few days a week. I smiled as I opened the door and stepped into a new part of my life. The same, cute Asian lady was at the desk on the left and as I closed the door I told her who I was.

"I'm a new intern for Premiere. I'm supposed to start today."

"Hello again," she said. "I'm glad you were hired."

"Thank you, thanks a lot."

"My name's Sandi. Your supervisor wanted me to have you wait out here until nine."

"Okay."

I turned to sit down and noticed a young lady already sitting there. "Are you an intern too?" I asked.

"Yes, I am. Nice to meet you."

And so we talked to each other where we were waiting and soon another female intern showed up and sat with us and Sandi called someone on the phone. Within a minute Ms. Krause came back and greeted us and had us all go into the conference room and then welcomed us and explained the details of the job and asked us if we had any hours that we couldn't work. I was open to any work schedule, though I knew for sure that I would have to get one if not two other jobs in order to support myself. And in the back of my mind I knew I would have to borrow money from my parents and cut back on food and not have money for extra things, but I was very happy about the internship and couldn't have cared less about those other things.

It rained a lot on this third day of January, my first day on the job, and I loved it, loved the rain and clouds and cold outside. I loved my new co-workers there too. I loved my boss and all the movie posters on the wall. There wasn't anything that I didn't love there.

"Let me stop here and give you all a chance to move your cars," said Ms. Krause. "There's some free parking on the street about two blocks west and north of here."

"Great, I was getting worried about the meter where I had parked," I said.

The three of us interns went outside and moved our cars to where they wouldn't be towed away and this made all of us feel a heck of a lot better.

The first week on the job was spent just getting to know the routine and what we were required to do. Our biggest responsibility was transcribing the interviews of the reporters and editors and this was great because the interviews were with cool people like film directors, writers, actors, and producers. And it was all about movies and stars and world premieres of movies and all of that stuff and I loved every minute of it.

We also did other things like answer the phones, send faxes, prepare documents for mailing, distribute the mail, prepare for meetings, and anything else that needed to be done. And in the context of the movie and Hollywood business, everything was interesting and fun and exciting and I regretted that I only worked a day and a half each week.

One time one of the reporters, a man named Fred S. who was the coolest person and most down-to-earth writer ever, asked me to do some work for him and I was more than happy to oblige. He sent me to some local courthouses to get information on a court case between a super-famous movie star and his wife, and I guess they were getting divorced because they were disclosing bad things about each other and it was a big mess. So I got as many documents as I could and brought them back to him. And later he had me do this again, on another case, and I drove to Van Nuys and found the courthouse and got as much info as I could but it wasn't enough for what he needed for his article and I was completely disappointed with myself for not doing a better job, for not helping him as much as I could for his cool article about the cool life of some cool people who were being offered cool sums of money for the cool story about their cool life. So I apologized to Fred S. and swore that I would never let him down again, and I never did.

And because I had aspirations in the entertainment industry, I paid attention at work and found phone numbers I could use and addresses and names of casting agencies and directors, and I tried to remember as much as possible in case I needed them later on, in case I wanted to make something of myself, in case I wanted to make it big.

Work went on and I survived week to week and I always wondered where I would get the money for the next week's rent and sometimes I had just enough for rent and nothing else, nothing at all, but this didn't bother me, not a bit, because of the neighborhood where I lived and the opulence all around me and how I didn't seem so poor at all even though I was. I never planned on living in Beverly Hills. It just happened to be the only place I could find at such short notice that had a room available on a week-to-week basis.

I got to know Sandi more and talked to her as much as possible at work. She told me how she had started at Premiere as an intern and then moved to an administrative position. She had graduated from UCLA and had relatives up in the Bay Area. I liked her a lot and thought she was just perfect, until something happened one day. I had walked to a local restaurant for lunch and was heading back to the office when Sandi saw me and asked if I wanted a ride with her, and of course I agreed. She had a really nice BMW but I would have ridden with her if she had been on a bicycle.

"Where's your car?" she asked.

"Oh, down the street. I just felt like walking to lunch today because it wasn't that far away." Actually, I was trying to save my gas because I couldn't afford more of it.

"I do that sometimes. What kind of car do you have?"

"A Datsun."

"You drive a Datsun?" she asked, seemingly stunned that anyone owned such a vehicle.

"Well, my Volvo is in the shop," I said, in such a way that it seemed obvious, to me at least, that I was just joking.

"Oh, that's okay then. Volvo's are good and really safe."

I wasn't sure what to say next. I hadn't expected her to take me seriously about the Volvo. I didn't like how superficial and materialistic she seemed but I wasn't going to cause any more confusion by saying that I hadn't been serious about the Volvo. I just let it be and we went back to work and I continued to like her and want to be with her, though I was severely disappointed in her.

4

My tiny apartment on the second floor of the complex in Beverly Hills was just fabulous. Sure, I barely had enough space to move around, but I had what I needed: a kitchen area, a bed, a bathroom, and a small desk area. The rent was a hundred and twenty-five a week and this was perfect because I never had to come up with a large sum of money at any particular time. There was no way I would be able to do that.

And the neighborhood, as you can imagine, was absolutely perfect. Every street was beautiful and the homes were all incredible and the lawns were perfectly trimmed and of the darkest green, and Rodeo Drive was six blocks away and I went there a lot but never bought anything. There were palm trees all around and my apartment complex was grand, with ivy dangling all over, and lush, green, big plants hanging here and there, and flowers and tall trees stretching to the sky, and lovely fragrances being exuded from the plants. Man, it was a perfect place to live, except for the tiny, tiny apartment.

I was really desperate for money after a month in L.A. so I signed up at a temporary employment agency and they gave me an assignment as an extra for a talk show. This was fine by me because I was able to eat between the taping of the shows, for they had free pizza and soda for the cast, crew, and anybody else.

A week later I got a call from Lorrie and I couldn't believe that I hadn't called her yet. After all, it was because of Paul's kindness that I had gotten to my interview on time and was able to wear a suit jacket.

"I'm sorry," I said. "I've just been working and trying to find work and barely having any money to do anything."

"Would you like to go up to Cal Arts with me and Paul?" she asked. "There's a dance show we would like to see."

"Oh yes, that would be nice."

"Okay, we'll pick you up at seven."

"I'll wait outside then."

"All right."

I gave them my address and later met them out front. On the way to the university, I talked all about my job as an extra and my work at the magazine.

We watched the play, which was more of a dance show, and then afterward we went to a restaurant.

"You know, I could imagine you as a magazine writer," said Lorrie's boyfriend Paul.

"It would be nice," I replied. "I could sure use that kind of money."

And then Lorrie and Paul started talking about different things and I began to dislike them altogether and hoped that the evening would end as soon as possible and I couldn't believe that I ever liked them in the first place.

"Hey, I saw Kevin last week," said Lorrie. "You remember him?"

"Of course. We hung out quite a lot in college, until he moved south again."

"I was delivering something to a studio and he was walking from one building to the next so I honked and we chatted for a while."

"Did you get his phone number?" I asked.

"Yeah, you want it?"

"Sure. Man, I haven't talked to him in a long time."

"Let me get it for you." She wrote it down on a napkin and I resolved to call him the next day.

I did call him and we talked on the phone and he invited me over to his apartment in Santa Monica to catch up on old times. He was the same old Kevin, always funny and always laughing and always a great guy to be around and I knew he had lots of friends. It was strange being with him again, given how we had known each other at the university and how long ago that seemed to me.

One night he took me to a club he knew about and it was an improvisation group and they seemed funny enough but I didn't like it very much and was glad when we left. He drove me back to my place at about two in the morning and on the way we talked about lots of things like our time in college and the girl we knew very well, the girl named Claire.

"Hey, she lives on the east coast," I said. "It's gotta be morning there by now. You want to call her? I have her number."

"It's too early," he said. "We'll wake her up."

"Well, come up and see how tiny my apartment is and then we'll make a decision."

He came up to my room and saw how impossibly small it was.

"Is that her in the picture?" he asked.

"Oh yes." There was a picture of Claire on my wall, the one from our New Year's Eve celebration and party so long ago.

"Who's that guy?"

"I don't know," I lied. Of course it was me but nobody could tell that because only part of the back of my head was visible. Someone had taken a picture while the two of us were on the floor. "Let's call her."

"I'd rather not."

"Come on, you two were best friends. She'd love to talk to you."

"Still."

I decided to do it. I missed her terribly and had to speak to her again, no matter what time it was. I dialed and waited.

"May I speak to Claire?" I said when someone answered. The voice on the end of the line told me to wait.

"Someone's going to get her," I told Kevin.

"Hang up, hang up now."

And then she was on the phone and man I was the happiest person on the planet and almost didn't know what to say.

"Hello Claire, it's Darrin Atkins, from college."

She said hello.

"Sure, I know it's late, well, probably early there. It's just after two here."

She asked if I was still in Beverly Hills. I had sent her a letter a month earlier, right after I had arrived in the city.

"Yes, and I have someone here who wants to talk to you."

I motioned for Kevin to come to the phone and he hesitated at first and then took the receiver.

"Hello," he said. Then he listened. "Yes, it's Kevin. This call wasn't my idea. I tried to get him not to call you."

Getting Kevin on the phone with Claire was a good idea, I believed, because I knew how well they used to get along and I figured Kevin could keep in touch with Claire better than I could, given my previous history with her and how things had developed between us. I was jealous of him and his relationship with Claire, but I needed a good excuse for calling Claire so late and I figured this was as good as one could be.

Before I knew it they finished talking and exchanged phone numbers and hung up. Then Kevin left and I was alone and slept well with my thoughts and memories of Claire dancing around in my head. I slept just fine, I did indeed.

5

The job at the magazine was great and the people and work was always entertaining. There were always producers and directors on the phone and our reporters were always talking about the interviews they just had and what was going on in town. Someone mentioned something that finally helped me understand the meaning of the word Hollywood.

"Hollywood doesn't refer so much to the actual city," she said to me. "It refers more to the entertainment industry. You know, there are actually no movie studios in Hollywood. Sony's in Culver City, Fox is in Century City, and on and on. Hollywood really means all the studios and companies and agencies and everything else."

"Oh, that makes sense now. Thanks."

Of course the reporters were always under pressure to write their articles and meet deadlines and have things finished right away. And often the interns would feel that pressure and be forced to transcribe something right away or go to Beverly Hills and find some rare book or article or movie information and rush it back to the office for them, and this was all great and fun and exciting and I loved it all.

One time I was working at the desk and it was really quiet in the afternoon, I guess most of the reporters were on assignment somewhere, and I was sorting the mail and minding my own business. Then, suddenly, one of the reporters, an attractive woman named Rachel, threw open her office door and stormed outside and into the little corridor and rushed up and down the hallway as she screamed "fuck! fuck! fuck!" about a hundred times. I tried very hard not to look at her or act surprised because I didn't want her cussing at me. Just as suddenly, she went back to her office and slammed her door behind her and then it was quiet again and I wondered if it had happened at all.

Another time I was using the copy machine to copy some pages of studio addresses and phone numbers, a task I wasn't supposed to be doing because it was for personal use to help me in my career later on, when the copy machine jammed and I didn't know how to fix it.

"Let me help you with that," said my boss who happened by at just that moment.

I grew tense and nervous and hoped that she wouldn't ask me what I was doing. She opened the copier and pulled out the jammed paper.

"There," she said. "It should work now."

"Thanks a lot," I said sheepishly. She walked away and I felt relieved and swore that I wouldn't do that again.

Then there was this one lady in the advertising department who always looked great and wore wonderful, lovely clothes, and I never talked to her because she seemed so perfect. But one day she showed up without her makeup on and, I hate to say it, she was ugly as hell and just my luck she came over to talk to me about something and I had to force myself not to act different at all and to just be normal because I'm sure she was aware that she wasn't wearing makeup and looked different because of that fact, that she didn't look nearly as good as she usually did. And I was happy that I never had to wear so much makeup and make myself all pretty like that because it was surely a heck of a lot of work and I had enough to think about as it was.

Then I was working one day and there was a fire drill and all of us had to head outside and it was the best time ever, just hanging out on the sidewalk with all of these reporters and writers who wrote about the Hollywood film industry.

That day I read something in the paper about a special tribute to Steven Spielberg that night by the American Film Institute. It was to be held in Beverly Hills so I decided to go there after work and maybe see some celebrities. It was close to my place so I walked there in the early evening. I walked inside the hotel and over to a small section that was cordoned off for spectators like me. And then I waited and soon every major celebrity in Hollywood walked right by me and I was stunned to be just a few feet away from Jack Nicholson, Warren Beatty, Tom Hanks, Sally Field, Danny Glover, Charo, and every other celebrity that you could possibly imagine. All right there in front of me. And it was just amazing to me, it really was.

My brother and his wife and kids came down to go to Disneyland later in the week and stopped at my place to visit one night. I told them all about the celebrities I had seen and how close I had been to them and how I had forgotten to take my camera.

"Are you working now?" he asked me.

"I'm still at the magazine, but only for about a few months more. That's when my internship ends."

"What after that?"

"I've applied to work at this new Wolfgang Puck cafe."

"Really?" he asked, surprised. "Would you mind getting him to sign one of his cookbooks for me?"

"I'll try. Of course I have to get the job first."

"I'd be grateful."

"Sure, no problem."

Then we chatted some more about other things and I gave them a couple recent issues of the magazine with my name on the inside, listed with the other interns and underneath all of the big people in the company. And they were happy with where I worked and thought it was cool and I agreed with them. And then all of us laughed at my impossibly small apartment and at how much I paid for something like that.

6

One day I was at work and one of the reporters was leaving on an assignment.

"Where are you going?" I asked him.

"A photo shoot with Sandra Bullock. I have to write a short article about it."

"Wow, that sounds really great." And of course it did sound great.

"It's okay."

I had read that Ms. Bullock was doing some promotion work for a new movie she was in called "Speed" with Keanu Reeves and Dennis Hopper. I had actually spoken to Mr. Hopper when he called the week before to be interviewed by my boss. Well, actually, all I said to him was, "One moment. I'll transfer you." But still, I had talked to Dennis Hopper and that was true.

I went back to work and thought about all this and wondered what "Speed" would be about and when it would be in theaters. I got the mail later that day and dropped off some of it to Sandi. Our mailboxes were close together and often her department's mail was accidentally put into our box and vice versa.

"I got some free passes yesterday to see a new movie," she said before I went back to my desk.

"Would you happen to have an extra one?" I asked.

"Yes, I have four. Two of my friends said they would go so I have one more."

"I'd love to go," I said, inviting myself.

So we arranged the evening together with her friends and she told me what time and where to meet her and the others. The free tickets were for an early screening of a romantic movie and of course I was happy to go without paying, especially given my severe lack of funds, and I was more than willing to do anything with Sam. She was as cute as can be.

When the evening came I sat next to Sandi on her left and her friends sat on the other side.

"This is my last free evening for a while," I said to her.

"Why's that?"

"I'm become involved with a production of Hamlet in Culver City. It's on a volunteer basis, just building sets and stuff, but I'll be doing sound during the show. So I have to go to the rehearsals and performances."

"I didn't know you did that kind of stuff."

"I don't do it a lot. I really should be working somewhere but this is more fun."

Then we watched the movie and I enjoyed sitting next to her and hoped that we would be able to go out again some time in the future. Sandi was fabulous, though often I thought about what she had said about my car and that kind of got to me.

7

I started work at the Wolfgang Puck cafe in Manhattan Beach and it was a brand new building in a location close to the beach. We were able to sample all the food and even the oven-roasted pizzas which I loved quite a bit. I liked my co-workers because a lot of them were actors and writers too. In fact, one pretty girl was close friends with a girl who was featured in an article of Premiere that month, so of course that was very cool and me and this girl got along really well at work and everything was grand.

Wolfgang showed up for the grand opening of the restaurant, of course, and all of us got to meet him. He signed some autographs for people and I knew this was the perfect opportunity to get his signature for my brother. I purchased one of his cookbooks from the person at the register and then I took it over to Wolf.

"Could you sign it for a customer?" I asked.

"Sure. What's the name?"

"Steven."

Then he signed it and gave it back to me and I got what I wanted. I wrapped it up in a box and sent it to my brother and it was just what he wanted, though he never actually tried to make any of the recipes inside the book, for whatever reason.

Wolf was always on some talk show or at a grand premiere of another cafe or restaurant and we hardly ever saw him after the first month of business. He even started being the chef for the Academy Awards and was so successful that he does it all the time now.

Pretty soon I was only working at the restaurant on the weekends, because I knew that I needed to get a full-time job and knew I wouldn't be able to survive on the small amount of income from the restaurant. I started searching for work while I still had two weeks left at the magazine.

In early May I realized that my internship would end soon and I was grateful that I had made it that far, that I hadn't run out of money for rent or had to move somewhere else.

I was friends with a young writer at Premiere named Kristin and she was really cool and had been an assistant director on one of Steven Spielberg's friends.

"Do you have a favorite actor?" she asked me one day.

"No," I said. "But I have a favorite producer."

"Who?"

"Kathleen Kennedy," I said. "She's so great. She's produced lots of fabulous movies and she's supportive of other people and she's so very cute."

"Really?" she asked me. "How do you know this about her?"

"I read it in the back issues and I even copied some pictures of her. Here they are." I showed them to Kristin.

"You know, I used to work with her."

"No way." I was astounded.

"Seriously."

"Wow."

And then we went back to work and I kept dreaming of Kathleen and kept adoring her pictures. Every time I saw Kristin she would ask about my infatuation with Ms. Kennedy and remind me that she was married to a director, but I didn't mind because there was nothing wrong with just adoring someone.

Before my last day of work, the head writers planned a party for the interns at a local restaurant and of course we all went and it ended up being the most wonderful night ever because I was with people I admired and we talked about the movie industry and talked about writing and reporting and I just couldn't believe how perfect it was.

On my last day of work, Kristin came over to me and gave me something in an envelope.

"Oh, I didn't get you anything," I said.

"Well, I still have a job here. You don't."

"Oh yeah." I opened the package and it was an 8x10 photo of Kathleen Kennedy, my favorite producer.

"Thank you, thank you so much," I said, completely surprised. "I can't believe it."

"Look what she wrote."

I looked at the picture and it was signed: Best wishes Darrin, Kathleen Kennedy.

"Wow," I said. "This is incredible. Thank you a lot."

"She was happy to do it. Maybe one day you two will meet."

"I hope so, I really do."

And so I finished up my work and that was my last day at Premiere magazine and I couldn't believe how fast the time had gone and how now it was over and I didn't know what I was going to do.

8

I kept searching and searching for full-time work and finally found a job at Los Angeles International Airport as a skycap, or at least the closest thing to that kind of position. My job was to help passengers with getting a cab, help them with their luggage if they needed it, and give general information about terminals and airport facilities to passengers and other personnel as needed. I had to quit the restaurant job and that was fine by me. I had had enough of that place and I couldn't coordinate the two schedules.

I worked the evening shift from four to twelve-thirty and this was fine by me. I started to like the job because of the cab drivers, who were usually either Russian or Arabian, my co-workers, who were virtually all African-American, and the passengers at the airport, of every nationality imaginable.

I was making money again, but just barely enough to survive. The skycap position was just to make money and I knew I wasn't going to be there for very long, that it wasn't related to any sort of career. I worked hard, though, and helped people with their luggage, and kept busy, and chatted with the cab drivers, and saw a celebrity now and then, and loved the craziness that occurred at the airport on Friday and Sunday evenings, when LAX was jam-packed with people and luggage and buses and cars and limos and motorcycles and vans and shuttles and more and more people, nearly to the point of absurdity.

In early June my parents came down to visit me and it was good to have their company. We did some tourist things and they stayed in a hotel in Santa Monica. I told them about my job at the airport and how I didn't like it.

"You know, you can always come home," said my mother. "We've still got your room ready."

And it was nice to know this because I was certainly growing tired of my life in L.A. and I was very nearly out of money. Before they left I had some trouble with my car and my father said he would work on it as I worked that night. So then we were in a rush to get me to work because traffic was exceptionally bad.

"Follow that cab," I said to my father as we got close to the airport. I knew that the cab was mostly likely headed for the taxi waiting lot which was where I started my shift and clocked in every day,

"I've always wanted to say that," said my mother.

"Go ahead, there's a different one. They're all going to the same place."

"Follow that cab," said my mom with gusto.

And during the next day we went to Universal Studios and to the Universal Citywalk and had fun and did all kinds of other things. We thought about going to Spago and then changed our mind because none of us were into that whole lifestyle. Soon they went home and I thanked them for coming and, after they left, I figured that I probably would go home soon and move back up north.

The next few weeks were crazy at the airport because I really learned a lot about what was going on there, at least with the people with whom I worked. We were instructed when we first started and reminded every week not to be nice to the cab drivers and to stay away from them because of the temptation for bribery and kickbacks.

Since the skycaps were often asked by passengers where they could get a cab to a certain destination, maybe one far away, the skycaps could direct these passengers to a certain cab and that driver would get a large fare. And if he did that, the driver would reciprocate in kind and petty soon the whole orderly system would be chaos with drivers and skycaps doing favors for each other.

"If any driver gives you money, we will give you a hundred dollars if you call us immediately and show it to us," we were informed by our supervisors.

But a skycap would have to be crazy to do this, unless it was his last day, because then the drivers would hate you and the other skycaps would too because nobody likes a rat, nobody at all.

Everyone could see some corruption going on and the Russian drivers got a kick out of it because they would say things like, "We escape the corruption in Russia and move here and find more corruption at the airport. You can't get away from it."

There was always talk of paybacks and favors and I shied away from friendly cab drivers because I knew what they wanted me to do for them and I knew what they wanted to start. And one time I fell for it and thought that a driver liked me as a person and a week later he got made at me when I wouldn't direct a big fare to him. So that ended everything for sure and I wasn't friendly any more. Some skycaps did favors and made extra money this way and nobody said anything because nobody wanted to cause any trouble. It was just the way of our little world and it wasn't going to change any time soon.

Slowly I grew tired of this because the drivers became more aggressive in their buyout attempts and I could feel the tensions around me as I could see and detect more of what was happening right under me, and I didn't like it at all. There's something about bribery, corruption, and kickbacks that doesn't make me feel so comfortable, but then maybe that's just me.

9

I saw Sandi for the last time about two weeks later. I had missed her a lot and wanted to say good-bye so I called her up and we decided to meet for lunch at a Chinese restaurant. She was leaving her job for a better, higher-paying position at another magazine. It was a nice lunch and it was great being in her company again.

"What have you been doing?" she asked me.

"Well, I have this job at the airport as a skycap. It's not a career move, just something to make some money."

"I bet it's interesting there."

"That it surely is. In my spare time I've been doing some writing."

"What kind? A screenplay?"

"No, nothing like that. They're short stories. One's about this couple on a train and they're scientists and develop this potion that accidentally sends them back in time a few hours."

"Wow. I wish I could write."

"I saw an ad for a position at The Hollywood Reporter," I said. "So I'm going to apply for that."

"Really? That would be wonderful. I don't know anyone there, but I'll ask around where I work and see if they know anybody. If they do, I'll let you know."

"Thanks very much. I could sure use any help like that."

"It's really a small town, at least in terms of magazine work. Everybody knows everyone else or has worked with them before."

I looked at Sandi and just adored her because she was so cute and wonderful and I wanted to keep her in my life forever. We drove back to her place and talked some more and I walked her to her door.

"I'm really going to miss you," I said as I hugged her.

"Keep in touch," she said.

"I will," I promised. "Bye." And I did keep in touch as much as I could but time went on and she got busy in her career and I got busy in mine and I never saw her again.

I tried very hard to stay in L.A. There were openings at a trucker magazine and I thought for sure I had a good chance at a job there, especially after I had an interview. After waiting a week and not receiving a call, I called the lady with whom I had interviewed.

"I'm sorry," she said. "We decided to go with someone else."

"Well, thanks for the interview. I've decided to move back up north."

"If you're ever in L.A. again, drop me a line and I'll see if we have any openings."

"Thanks a lot. I'll do that." I wasn't sure if she was sincere or not but it didn't matter too much at the time.

And I even applied at and was interviewed by The Hollywood Reporter and I just knew that it would have been the coolest job ever if I had gotten it, but they never called me back and I wasn't offered a position and at the end of the month of June I decided it was time to head home.

I didn't want to work at the airport job any more and on my last night, when I was going to be off the next two days, I decided to quit and go home. I turned in my uniform the next day and resigned. Then I packed up my stuff and moved out.

I had lasted a lot longer in L.A. than I thought that I would, given my lack of money and job restraints and small income. But I had completed my internship at Premiere and that was what I had moved to L.A. to do and I was quite happy and content with the experience and everything had worked out in the end.

When I got home I took a break for a while and then started applying for work. After I was working for a while, I got involved with the local cable access channel and started developing a half-hour comedy show. I got a letter from Sandi and she said that she got the job at Los Angeles magazine, where I had interviewed for an internship but declined because I didn't want to intern any more. About a month later I got a postcard from her when she was on a trip to the Bahamas, and of course I wanted to be there with her and I imagined how nice it must be to be able to go to the Bahamas and drive a BMW and make fun of cars that other people drove. I missed Sandi a lot and wished that things had developed between us, but then I thought of how materialistic she was and I was happy the way things had turned out. I was home again and everything was boring in comparison to what had happened to me in L.A. and so I started saving money so I could go back. I would make sure I had a lot of money for the next time I tried my luck in L.A. and I couldn't wait for that day to came and it couldn't come fast enough for me.

PART 2

Koreatown, Los Angeles

I

It was easy driving back to L.A. and I soon realized how much I had missed everything, missed the beaches, missed the palm trees, missed the movie industry. I didn't know where I was going to leave or work or live. I just knew that I wanted to be back in the great city of Los Angeles and that there were still some things that I wanted to do there, that I had left too soon before, that I had a lot more to do with movies and films and the whole entertainment industry.

I stopped near where I used to live, at a grocery store on the west side of Century City and on that other side of that big hill. I knew that I could go back to where I used to live, that there might be an opening in that apartment complex in Beverly Hills, but that wasn't what I wanted at all. I wanted a change. I wanted to live somewhere else, somewhere different, but somewhere that was interesting. I found some apartment ads in the paper and used my map and drove around town in an attempt to find them. I wanted to find a place right away.

I drove over to Culver City and found an apartment complex and got out and tried to find the manager's office but nobody was around. I did find someone who lived next to the manager.

"I'm interested in one of the apartments," I said to her.

"Come back in a couple hours," she replied. "He'll be here then."

"Okay, thanks." I had some other places on my list. They were over by Westwood and UCLA so I started off there. On the way I passed by the street I used to take in Culver City that led to that theater group where I had volunteered during that Shakespeare play. I made it to Westwood but had trouble finding the apartments, and then when I did they seemed too crowded and I had a negative feeling about it all so I decided not to go there. Then I drove around some more but couldn't find the next places at all. I stopped for lunch and then tried hard to think of what I was doing. I wanted to find a place right away and I had a good amount of money, but I didn't want to use it all at once by paying the first and last month's rent as well as a deposit. I needed a place like before, where I could pay week by week if I wanted to. That was the biggest thing that I cared about. I didn't want to drive around anymore because I had done that for three hours and the thick, congested L.A. traffic was getting to me because I wasn't used to it at all.

Finally I found an ad for a hotel building and it had the option of renting by the week or month and they had meals available and mentioned something about it being a good place for students. I liked it and decided to try and find it. I located it on the map and it was pretty far from Century City and the west side but that wasn't too big of a deal. I headed east and drove for a while and then found the street and went down it but when I got to the end, where it stopped, I couldn't find the building at all. I looked all around but it just wasn't there. Something had to be wrong because the ad was in that day's paper so it had to be right. I looked on the map again and the was relieved when I saw that the street continued a few blocks east. There was a giant property and old historic hotel that broke up the street. I found my way around it and soon I was on the other side and then I found the apartment building.

I parked and looked hard at it. It wasn't in a nice neighborhood and the building didn't look glamorous at all. It was a very dull gray with streaks from years of rain, but there was a great big sign outside that said that it had weekly rates that included regular meals and this appealed to me right away. I made the decision quickly that this was not my place of residence.

I locked my car and went to the entrance. There was a big awning out front and I walked under it on my way inside. I looked around and saw some chairs on both my left and right and then there was the hotel desk up in the middle of the lobby and to my left. The desk was semi-circular and a man stood there and there was a door behind him that seemed to lead to an office. I liked the place and went over to the counter.

"I'm interested in staying here," I said. "You have weekly rates, right?"

"Sure, weekly, monthly, daily"

"I'd like to get a week."

"Okay. Let me get the paperwork." He pulled out a big ledger and a sign-in book. "I need you to fill this out." I started to do so as he talked about the place. "Your room will be cleaned daily unless you say otherwise. You get breakfast and dinner and there's a sign out front, over there behind you, that says when the hours of the cafeteria are. There's a phone in your room." Then he told me the cost for the week and I paid it. "Here's your key. You're lucky because we just recently stopped asking for a key deposit."

"That's a good sign," I said. Of course I was looking for good signs.

"There you go."

"What about mail?"

"Are you going to stay here a while?"

"Maybe."

"If you do we have a slot for your room and you can just have your mail sent here and you can pick it up any time."

"Oh, okay. Thanks."

"You're welcome."

I walked to my right to where the stairs were located and then I followed them up to the third floor. I followed the sign, turned right and my room was the second one on the left, number 323. I opened it up and stepped inside. There was a large bed in the center in the room and it faced a nice large dresser with a large television on it. There were two night stands on both sides of the bed and a desk and lamp on the right as I entered. I shut the door and sat down on the bed and realized that this was my home, this five-story apartment building in Koreatown, and I wondered if it was the right place, I wondered if things would go well for me there, and I wondered if I would be happy. I felt alone, all alone, and it was an awful feeling. I sat there for a while before I went outside to bring in my stuff. Later that day the clerk at the counter told me about the parking lot and how that was the safest place for my car.

2

I got settled after a few days and soon things were easier for me. I moved in all my stuff and had my computer on the little desk and I watched television from the comfort of my large bed. I had my meals downstairs in the cafeteria and I ate by myself and observed all of the other people who ate there and wondered about them and kept to myself.

Of course I needed a job and figured my best chance would be through a temporary service so I located one and applied. I figured I could get some money coming in as I looked for a more career-oriented position. The agency called me and informed me of a job at a library service down in a city called Downey. I accepted the assignment and found a map and realized that it was quite a distance away, that I would have to travel on three different freeways, but at least it was something and it didn't matter too much about everything else. I loved books and the fact that it had to do with a library made a lot of difference.

After the first week at this job, I remembered the lady at the trucker magazine and how she said that I could call her if I was ever in L.A. again and needed a job. I knew in my heart that she hadn't meant this, that it was just something nice for her to say given the fact that I hadn't been selected by her company at that time. I still had her name and I found the company again and was able to locate her extension in the company directory over the phone. I left her a detailed message about who I was and that

I was interested in applying for her company again. When I hung up I knew that it had been a waste of time and I wondered why I had tried at all.

I only lasted at the temp assignment at the library for two weeks because during this time I applied for a position with a business newspaper and they scheduled an interview for me the following week and I figured I had a real good chance at the job, and frankly I was tired of driving all the way down to Downey and much preferred the thought of driving to and working in Marine del Rey. Plus, I still had a lot of the money I had saved during the year when I was back in Stockton.

I went to the interview at the paper and waited in the lobby until my name was called. A woman greeted me and took me through the hallways.

"Sorry about the wait," she said. "It's a busy day around here."

"No problem," I said. I had no place else to go and I wanted to work at a newspaper again, even if the position was in customer service and not in the newsroom where I wanted to be.

"Our department manager is out of town this week," continued the woman, "so our assistant managers will interview you."

"Fine by me."

The preliminary interview was done a chubby man, in his late twenties I assumed, who seemed confident and upbeat and the questions he asked were relatively benign and I answered them with ease. The next two interviews were a bit more difficult, but I knew I had plenty of customer service experience and I had worked for other papers so I figured I was qualified for the position.

"It looks like a lot of your experience has slanted toward the writing or production side," asked on of the interviewers. "Are you sure you would be content in this department?"

"Oh, I'm not in a rush to be a writer. I like to have experience in other departments to be well-rounded. It would be nice if I got hired in the newsroom later on, but I'm not set on that as an absolute."

"Sounds good."

I hoped nobody would ask me about the dates when I worked at some of the companies I had listed, because I had stretched out the timelines to make myself appear more stable than I was. Simply put, I couldn't keep a job for very long, but I certainly didn't want a future employer to know that.

"Well, it looks like you're qualified," said the last interviewer. "We'll make a decision by the end of the week and call you on Monday of next week."

"Thank you. I look forward to working here."

I was led out of the company and I walked back to my car and took off for home. On the way I saw some signs for the airport, given Marina del Rey's proximity to it, and I thought back to my job there the year before.

3

Slowly I became familiar with the routines of the hotel and neighborhood and I noticed certain people all the time because they were residents there. My job search was in full force but I couldn't find anything for a full month and finally had to accept a temporary assignment far away. just so I would have some money coming in.

The food in the cafeteria was not so great, but it was food and it was paid far because its cost was included as part of the rent. I was paying my rent by the week until about the third week when the manager suggested that I pay by the month instead because it was less expensive that way, so I agreed and paid my first full month. I thought that I would look for a better place to live, but soon I met some people and made some friends and didn't want to leave, for a long while anyway.

At first my room was cleaned and my beds made daily, until I paid for a full month and then it was done just twice a week. And for a while I tipped the maid a little bit but only until enough time had passed to make me realize that I was paying enough.

There was a nice recreation room where some of the regulars hung out and had fun with the pool table and video games and television and big couches and nice lighting and cool views of the feet of passers-by. The big room was at a level lower than the outside sidewalk and all we could see of those walking by were their feet and part of their legs. There were signs printed in Korean all over the place and these were constant reminders, along with the local Korean people, that I was no longer in Beverly Hills.

One time, when I had a day off, I rode my bike downtown to go to the big city library and on the way I stopped and found myself on the set of a location shoot of the television series Alien Nation and I didn't even realize I was there or that there was anything going on until everyone around me looked like aliens with their shaved heads and heavy makeup.

Because of my free time on the weekends and my lack of friends, I spent a lot of time in the library, looking through genealogy books and civil war records, and found out that I had had relatives on both the north and the south sides of the Civil War, in the union and the confederacy, and I thought this was really cool and interesting.

Soon I started to meet all kinds of people and talked to them in the lobby and in the recreation room, replete as it was with video games, pool table, and a big-screen television. The first person I really got to know was Lugo. He was a short, Mexican guy with braided hair, and he was great fun to be around and loved movies, loved being in them, and always talked with a great energy and everybody liked him.

The first thing we did together was walk to the new subway extension that was opening near the hotel, along Wilshire Boulevard. It was an extension of the red line and there were free rides on it all weekend so of course we took advantage of this and we go there early and made sure we were on the first public ride to the end of the new line, and this extension was a big thing and there were reporters covering it and Lugo and I enjoyed the subway ride and thought the new line was great and we talked about the drilling through the mountains of the subway line that was in production there, that would open a few years later and go all the way to Hollywood.

"Where do you work?" asked Lugo one day as we were eating in the cafeteria downstairs.

"I don't know."

"What?"

"I mean, I just quit this one job in Downey, but I think I'll get this job a this paper in Marina del Rey, over by the airport."

"I've been there before as an extra. You should do it with me. You can make all kinds of money."

"I've done it before," I said. "I need something related to my career."

"What's your career?"

"Well, I want to be a reporter so this job at the paper is in the right field, but not the right department but I can work my way there. I used to work at Premiere, the movie magazine."

"Why did you leave? I would not leave."

"It was just an internship."

"What does that mean?" he asked.

"An internship is, well, it's just for a set period of time, like five months. It's usually for students even though I wasn't one at the time. It was minimum wage but the experience, that's why I was there."

"Oh."

"Wanna play some pool?"

"Sure."

I went and left a deposit for the balls and came back and we played for a while and eventually Dave and Jose showed up and all of us had a good time together and it was fun.

4

Finally I saw an ad in the paper for a job in the customer service department at a business paper in a nice city near the airport. I sent in my resume and hoped for the best and luckily they called me and set up an interview and I was hired quickly.

There was a full month of training required and we needed every day of this because there was so much to learn about the company and about the different printing locations and delivery routes and everything else involved in a daily paper.

Workers in some departments of the paper were required to disclose their financial holdings before they were hired and if they owned stocks and in which companies, so that there wouldn't be conflicts of interest between what they reported. Also, they were required to disclose their holdings when they were terminated or quit.

The new employees usually went out to eat to lunches at cafes in Marine del Rey near the water, or we brought our own lunches when we hadn't got paid for a while.

I became quick friends with a tall, attractive, light-skinned black guy who had come to L.A. because he had the money to do so, because of winning over ten thousand dollars on a game show. I agreed to pick him up for work every day and shouldn't have done this because often he took his time in the morning which caused us to be late, which in turn caused me to have some bad days.

The job went well for a while and I did my best and worked hard, but then things started to converge, and some of us were almost transferred to the telemarketing department, which we were adamantly against, and we were lied to a lot about the direction of the company and about some new systems that were being tried, which we were told was customer service but was actually outbound calls designed as foot-in-the-door techniques aimed at renewing customers' subscriptions, and I knew this because at one time, despite my misgivings, I had worked at a telemarketing firm and learned a lot of their tricks.

But this was steady income at a good wage and I did my best to dress well and perform well and keep my eyes on any in-house openings that might open in the newsroom and for which I had be qualified, though none ever came up.

5

People were always coming and going at the hotel and that was why I loved it there so much. In my first few months there, smoking was still allowed in the lobby and there was even a smoking vending machine. This was before the big California laws were enacted in California that prevented indoor smoking. Now I didn't smoke at all but some of my friends did and I didn't mind their smoke. I would just hang out in the front part of the lobby, near the entrance, and sit on the chairs they had there and people would smoke and I would chat with them. Lugo would smoke and tell me all about his work as an extra and these were very cool times indeed.

This was the best place to be, down in the lobby, because it was a constant hub of activity, what with new students coming and checking in, and tourists stopping in for a day or two, and always people doing this or that, a pretty, sexy woman arriving by herself and turning heads, people asking the clerk for directions to Hollywood and Mann's Chinese Theater, a group from Korea, this man from the Ivory Coast, a cabload of Germans, and on and on. Oh how I loved hanging out in the lobby when I first started living at the hotel, when people could smoke down there, when that smoking helped people socialize and talk and share their worldly knowledge. It would be different at the beginning of the new year when smoking laws were enacted and all of that was gone.

And then I hung out with Lugo one day and his Asian friends came over to talk to him and so that's how I met them and they were all pretty cool and invited me over to their room for drinks that very night and we got along very well. I really liked this one guy who I nicknamed Bruce because he looked so very much like Bruce Lee, though of course my friend was Japanese and Bruce Lee wasn't.

I hung out a lot with these guys and went to the beach with them and played beach volleyball and Bruce and I hung out a lot and I drove him to many places and we became great friends. And we complained of the hotel whenever we were with Lugo, we complained of the awful food and of how expensive it was to stay in the hotel, we complained of the horrible, giant cockroaches we saw in our rooms and even in the kitchen, and were aghast when we saw the mean, old, grouchy food server stamp to death some cockroaches right when we were eating and so we stopped eating, and we complained because of the rough neighborhood. But this was just for fun because in fact we liked where we lived and felt comfortable there and liked each other and none of us was planning on leaving soon.

We did as much as we could together and had fun and looked forward to the weekends when we could have more fun. There wasn't much of a language barrier between us. They knew some English and spoke it. Lugo and I didn't know any Japanese but still we hung out with our Japanese friends and drank in their room and laughed and communicated the best we could and had fun. We went to Little Tokyo to see some Godzilla movies together during a special festival and this was great except for a large contingent of immature American people at the showing who constantly and laughed and mocked the acting performances of the characters in the move and more than once I had to try and explain to my friends what these people were laughing at, and this was no fun at all. But then these friends, except Lugo, left on a big car trip to other parts of the country.

6

Lugo was funny because he got so excited about everything and had an unlimited amount of hope about his own prospects in the entertainment industry, as an extra and as an actor. One time he had a small part in a play and so I went to see him and it ended up being at this very tiny theater and only about seven people showed up to see the performance, and this didn't bother Lugo at all because, for whatever reason, he was eternally hopeful about Hollywood and what it could make of him, and I didn't mind his confidence, not one bit.

And he talked about his assignments as an extra and the difficulty he had in getting to all the studios in Los Angeles and up in the valley because he didn't have a car and had to take the buses and subway and light rail system.

Then he talked about how he had been asked to be an extra for the film production down in Mexico and he wanted me to go with him and this sounded great, but I didn't feel like moving out just yet so neither of us ended up going, though I realized later on that maybe I should have gone anyway.

"Come with me tonight," he said one evening. "I'm working as an extra on a movie down at the park."

"MacArthur Park?"

"Yeah, the one close by."

"I'm too tired. And I have to work tomorrow."

"It's easy, and I'm sure they'll hire you. They need people for the riot scenes."

But I said no and didn't go, not even after he said the movie was about a volcano in L.A.. I should have gone to this too.

"I was down there earlier today," I said. "And I saw someone filming something."

"Yes, they're filming all week."

But I recalled that the filming looked like it was being done by amateurs and I didn't want to waste my time, but this was another mistake on my part because they weren't amateurs at all. I should have gone to be an extra at this park, if not for the work as an extra then to see if it was true what Lugo had told me, that one could buy social security cards down there or passports or green cards or anything at all with the right amount of money.

Slowly I began to meet and develop some more friends, partly because Lugo knew other people. The first guy I met was this polite and friendly Japanese guy named Yasu, and he was the one to come up to me and ask if I would help him learn to speak English and do it correctly, and that he was willing to help me learn to read, write, and speak Japanese if I wanted that.

Then Yasu introduced me to his friend who lived in a room near Yasu's, and the friend's name was Hori and he loved to drink and party and watch porn films so of course I liked him a lot and he always invited me over to his room and we had great times, but he would leave after a few weeks and I would miss him a lot.

Through Yasu I met Harry who was a young film student from Denmark. He was okay in that he wanted to be a director of movies and had some ideas and was excited about his film classes at the college nearby. He was Caucasian like me and spoke English fluently so we had no problem becoming friends, especially after I informed him of my former employment at Premiere.

Then Lugo introduced me to two students from Spain who were remarkably different. David was a tall guy with lots of scruffy hair and an irritable, grouchy demeanor, though he was likable because he talked a lot. Jose was more quiet and was shorter than all of us and had a bald head, by choice because he liked to shave it. Both of these guys spoke with a noticeable Spanish accent, but both knew English well and spoke it to me when I was around. And even when they spoke Spanish, I could understand a little. And of course Lugo, Dave and Jose spoke Spanish a lot to each other, but often Lugo couldn't understand what Dave or Jose was saying and vice versa because of the differences in the language between Mexico and Spain. Neither Dave nor Jose was involved in film or the entertainment industry, so that was good, but both didn't mind talking about movies or listening to Lugo's tales. I would find out later that Dave disliked going to the movies and I only went to one showing with him and that was because we got some free passes and had nothing better to do.

Harry had two female friends in their early twenties who moved in at about the same time as me and him. The first one, the prettier of the two, was named Sylvia and she had nice blonde hair and a thin body and good complexion but she had an awful personality, very argumentative and bitter, so nobody liked her too much but tolerated her because she was nice to look at. The other girl was named Rebecca and she would become my great friend. She wasn't as pretty as Sylvia but more than made up for that with her warm personality and her consideration for others and willingness to talk and just be friendly. She was a photography major but ended up taking some film courses at the community college nearby because they were a part of her major and she thought they would be fun.

Throughout meeting all of these new friends, I continued to work at the newspaper and things progressed and some days were better than others and some days were worse. As the weeks passed there, I grew more fun of the religious lady who sat behind me at work, and I made up any excuse to talk to her and I ended up talking to her quite often, until one time when she, as a tam leader, and the co-manager pulled me off the phones and into a side room and discussed how I had been doing something wrong, how I had been submitting way too many requests for our postal service manager to investigate some delays in the papers getting to our customers. I felt betrayed by her when this happened, though I was to blame, and my interest in her lessened, mostly because I was embarrassed because of the mistakes I had made with all that. But I never stopped wanting to talk to her.

7

I got to know the manager of the hotel, a woman who had a young daughter, a husband who was always away, and they lived in a very large apartment upstairs on the fifth floor. This woman was nice and considerate, especially to the young students. She was also a strong-willed person and was always making sure the hotel was being run properly and effectively and one night took some pictures of one of the front desk clerks sleeping on the job. This woman was so nice that I figured she was reasonable and helpful and my suspicion would be confirmed at the end of the year.

Harry and I started getting to know each other and I let him borrow my video camera because he was a film student and wanted to practice on video first before shooting in film. The area where the hotel was located was unique and interesting and rough enough to be advantageous in terms of its location. A part of the film "Eye for an Eye" with Sally Field and Kiefer Sutherland was filmed at the cigarette and convenience store two blocks south from us, and part of the movie "Bound" was filmed in a hotel near ours.

So the first movies had their beginning, with Harry directing with the camera I had purchased when I had lived in Stockton and volunteered at the cable company. The first film was about shoes and Harry did a great job with the video camera and with a very flimsy topic and story, if you can call it that. Our next collaboration was much better.

The second video film we did was called "Out of Focus" and I acted in the lead, about a man who loses his glasses and everything he sees is out of focus, hence the title, and confusion erupts as he makes his way throughout his hotel in a difficult journey back to his room.

8

I admit now that I fell for Shizu, and liked her so much because she was so darned cute and upbeat and always had a nice smile. She was the prettiest of all the female students in the hotel and I became fond of her almost instantly.

I grew to be friends with the other Japanese students, namely Yasu and Sakura and Rumi and Hori, the alcoholic fun guy, because they all knew each other and often sat together and I couldn't help but get to know them.

Then one day things changed fast. I happened to sit with Rumi and Sakura one evening and I talked to them about little things and knew their English wasn't too good but they tried to speak to me and something had obviously gotten them excited because I had heard them talking about something a lot before I arrived.

"What's going on?" I asked. "What is it?"

Rumi seemed hesitant to say anything, but Sakura wasn't at all.

"You now Harry?" she asked me.

"Yes, the guy from Denmark."

"He and Shizu are a couple now."

"Oh, that's nice." Now really I was a bit jealous inside but not too much.

Rumi said something in Japanese to Sakura and then it was a little quiet. I figured Rumi didn't want to gossip and that was fine by me. I thought of something else and relayed what had happened to me at work that day at the paper.

Later that night I found Sakura downstairs in the lobby and talked to her some more.

"I'm really worried about Shizu," she said.

"Why?"

"Something's wrong with her. It's like she's obsessed with Harry. That's all she talks about and she doesn't go to school and stays up all night long."

"She'll get over it."

"It's not safe. She needs to sleep."

I laughed. "Maybe she really likes Harry."

"Too much. I'm sick of hearing about him. That's the only thing she talks about at dinner and I don't want to hear anything more about him. Always Harry, Harry, Harry."

That night I thought about al this and how obsessed Shizu seemed to be with Harry and it brought back some memories of someone I was obsessed about, someone I had never gotten over, someone great and fabulous in my life, a woman named Claire who had inspired me more than any other person on earth.

I was all confused emotionally and couldn't help but express myself in writing so I sat at my desk and wrote a poem of some sort about how I had lost Shizu, lost her in the sense that she was now Harry's girl, though I didn't let that be known in the lines. I said it in more vague terms and talked about how I had followed her and she had gotten on a bus and I couldn't see her anymore, though none of that had happened. Then I signed it and put it in an envelope and took it to the mailbox outside and mailed it to Shizu. No, I didn't hand it to the desk clerk so he could put it in her mail slot. I let it go through the postal system so some time would pass before it came back, so it wouldn't be so obvious that I was jealous of Harry and the fact that he had Shizu now.

Sakura and I got to know each other better and we especially enjoyed complaining about Harry and Shizu, about how immature they were with their puppy love. One night Sakura came to my place for a visit.

"Does she think we want to hear about it every day?" asked Sakura.

"I don't care about them," I answered.

"Me neither. It's sickening. Sometimes she'll talk about having sex with him, and say this right during dinner."

"That's awful. She shouldn't do that."

"I know."

"I mean, I like sex and like talking about it but I know when and where to do that."

"You say you have some beer?"

"Yes, I got it earlier today. I was lucky that the manager had this small refrigerator for me to rent."

"Are you going to drink?"

"Yes." I grabbed two beers and opened them and gave one to her as I drank mine and we chatted.

And soon enough we were flirting and smiling and looking at each other.

"You don't like the beer?" I asked her.

"I do, I just can't drink much because of my stomach. You have it."

"Okay." I took it and drank hers and was feeling the effects soon enough. And one thing led to another and we kissed and kissed some more.

I did lots of fun things with Sakura, like going to Universal Citywalk and eating at a Wolfgang Puck cafe there as I talked about having worked for one of those cafes out in Marina del Rey. We went to Beverly Hills often, for shopping and lunch and once to the Museum of Television and Radio.

A week later Sakura and I were in her room. "Where's Rumi?" I asked.

"She moved out."

"Why? Where to?"

"She and Shizu are real good friends so she wanted to move in with her."

"That's not nice of her, to leave you like that."

"It's okay, it's all right."

"I don't think so."

"She didn't like me as much and they knew each other from before."

And this was my opportunity. I could pretend that I wanted to maintain Sakura's relationship with Rumi and get a chance to spend time in the presence of Shizu.

"Let's go to their room and visit them."

"It's okay."

"No, it might be fun. Show them that it doesn't affect you."

"All right."

So then I set things in motion and we walked upstairs and Sakura led me to her room and we waited for a minute before knocking. Yasu had a room near Shizu's and at that time he happened to come out so we walked over and talked to him and soon enough he left to go visit Harry. Then we walked back to Shizu's door and I was about to knock on Shizu's door when she stopped me.

"Wait, they're talking," she said. She and I heard some voices speaking in Japanese. "It's Shizu and Rumi."

I watched Shizu as she listened to them, and she stood there and listened for a full five minutes and she grew disappointed and sad until soon she was about to cry.

"Let's go," she sobbed as she went back down the hallway. I knew something big had been said and I left with her, though part of me wanted to see Shizu hat night.

Sakura raced back to her room and I went inside to comfort her and see what was the matter. She went straight to her bed and jumped o it and started crying.

"What's wrong? What did they say?" I asked as I held her tight to me and she cried in my arms.

"They talked about me. I heard them say things."

"I'm sorry, this was all my idea."

"They don't like me. They said they don't think I'm pretty."

"I think you're pretty. Who cares what they think?"

"She said I'm no fun."

"You are fun. We have great times together."

"I hate them."

And this was how it was that night. Sakura cried and I held her and grew to hate Shizu and Rumi for having said what they said, for being so rude and mean, and I knew I was partly to blame.

One day Sakura came to my room.

"Are we dating officially?" she asked me.

I knew she wanted a commitment and a relationship and of course I felt obligated to give her one.

"Yes, of course."

This made her quite happy. "Oh good, I want to tell Yasu this because he doesn't believe me. So if he asks, you'll say this?"

"I wouldn't say anything else."

"Great, great." She stayed a while longer and we had a nice evening doing whatever we did but all I could think of was why in the hell would it matter to Yasu, why would Sakura need to tell him, and what did Yasu think of Harry and Shizu. I had a lot of questions but after a while I grew tired of them.

Sakura always wanted to spend the night in my room and in my bed, but I wasn't comfortable with this and never let her and didn't even know why I wouldn't allow it to happen.

"I like your room much better than mine," I said one day when I was visiting her there. "Maybe it's your dark wallpaper or how everything's laid out. It's just better. Maybe there's more space in here."

"I miss Rumi."

"It's okay, you've got more space here now."

"Maybe not for long. I might get another room mate."

"Sure, but until you do I hope we have lots of fun together with all this space and privacy."

"I hope so too."

And fun was exactly what we did have.

Then there was the time when I was in Sakura's room for a very long evening and we were doing what we were doing, if you know what I mean, and were as quiet as we could be.

Her phone rang a couple times but I wouldn't let her answer it. And there were knocks on her door but we were too occupied with ourselves to care. And more time passed and there were more calls and then there was some loud pounding on her door and we could hear Yasu and Shizu on the outside so finally we put our clothes back on and Sakura went to answer the door. I was out of view as they spoke.

"Are you okay?" asked Shizu.

"Yes, fine."

"Why didn't you answer before? I called a lot and was worried and went to get Yasu."

"Are you safe?" asked Yasu.

"I am."

And then Yasu and Shizu came into the place and saw me sitting on the bed and by the expressions on their faces I knew they realized what had been happening. Sakura shut the door and came back and the four of us tried to chat but it was quite uncomfortable. It seemed to affect Yasu the most because he hardly looked at me and just let his long hair flow in front of his face as he held his head in his hands. He was embarrassed and knew right away that they had interrupted us when we had been engaged in something awfully personal. They stayed and soon I excused myself.

"I'm going to go," I told Sakura. "Nice talking to you two," I said to Yasu and Shizu. And then I went back to my room and had a feeling that things between me Shizu and Yasu would be different from now on and indeed they were. They changed the most with Yasu. Shizu was still very polite and friendly with me and I came to like her even more because of her consideration and tact, though what she had said about Sakura to Rumi that one night still enraged me on an occasion or two. But only for a very short time and it always faded away.

9

My job at the paper continued, though things grew worse over time. I amused myself in my free time by helping Harry with his movies. I would hang out in his room and work on the short scripts for his films. he was taking film courses at the local community college and I would go there and hang out in the editing and viewing rooms as we planned what film we would use and how he would shoot the script and who the actors could be.

I tried to get along with him but sometimes he was just arrogant, or maybe I was jealous because of how much Shizu adored him, and I knew he needed a ride somewhere one night but I was mad at him and took off and drove to the beach and stayed away for as long as I could, long after he was supposed to be wherever.

But usually we got along well, because we were both interested in the projects. I told him about my work as a camera operator and film location scout and my former employment at Premiere. The first student film we worked on together that was called "Trouble on the Home Front" and it was about a couple, played by me and a young Mexican girl who was a friend of Harry's, and the trouble they have with the female character's brother who doesn't want them together. Dave played the brother. The film was short and started out with a romance between the couple and then the brother comes along and causes trouble. This film was a lot of fun to make because of the romantic angle and the chase scenes we filmed in the mountainous regions of Pasadena.

Most of the time the characters in Harry's films were portrayed by me, Dave, Jose, Yasu, or anyone else who was willing. This made things convenient, of course, and my encouragement and willingness to work with Harry surely moved things along faster than they would have gone otherwise.

The next film, related in story to the first, was called "No Harm Intended" and was a continuation of the first story. The same actors were used in the same roles but this time we focused more on shooting scenes inside or near the hotel and the hotel became one of the characters in the film.

And as we worked on these projects, I continued at my job and all of us tried to have as much fun and do things together like going to Santa Monica and the beach and Third Street and everywhere else. One cool evening, after a hot day earlier, we went to the beach at night and jumped into the water which felt absolutely perfect because the water was warm while outside it was a bit chilly. It was splendid but didn't last long because the beach patrol came and chased us out and said that we couldn't swim at night because of dangers posed by the rides. So we headed back to my car but on the way we stopped at McDonald's.

10

Then one day my Japanese friends returned from their cross-country trip and I had nearly forgotten all about them and had thought that they had moved away for good because I hadn't seen them for so long. I had since made new friends and now things seemed strange because my loyalties were divided between my new friends and the ones I had when I first got to the hotel. But it was great to see them again and they had drinking parties in their rooms and I went and hung out with them and Lugo and we had great times drinking sake and beer and whiskey and every other alcoholic drink. There was one thin and short Japanese girl among them and soon I discovered that she was now engaged to one of the guys there and I congratulated her and wished her the best.

I was in the cafeteria one day when Bruce came in, saw me, and walked right over to me.

"Darrin, we found this great apartment in a good neighborhood."

"Congratulations," I said as I noticed an application in his hands.

"It's so nice and big and not expensive and we want to live there."

"I hope you get it." I had a feeling what he was going to ask me and I hoped that he wouldn't.

"The only problem is that we're not residents here. We need someone to co-sign the lease."

I didn't want to say no right away, though I knew I would. "I don't have good credit," I lied. "I don't think I'd be much help."

"We've got plenty of money."

"I'm sure you do. Have you asked anyone else?"

"The front desk clerk, but he said no."

"I can't do it. It's a big risk because I'd be held liable if you leave."

"We won't. We're staying here."

"I know." I doubted him. Hell, I hadn't seen him for six weeks.

"We would really appreciate it."

"I can't. It's too risky. I barely know you." I could see him grow very disappointed and of course I wanted to help him, but I knew what he was asking even though he didn't. He was just a young guy, twenty at most, and his Japanese friends weren't much older. "I'm sorry, I want to help."

"Okay. I understand."

I didn't think that he did, but maybe it was good that someone else had said no to him before me, so he could at least see a pattern of some sort.

That Saturday I got a call from Lugo who was somewhere in the hotel. I could tell this by how many times the phone rang. I knew he had moved out of the hotel and was living elsewhere so I figured he was visiting Bruce and the others.

"You ready, Darrin?" he asked.

"For what?"

"The wedding. It's today."

"Really?"

"I told you the other night."

Maybe he had told me but I knew that I had drunk a lot and probably had forgotten. "I'll be downstairs in five minutes."

I got dressed very quickly in some nice clothes and raced downstairs and Lugo and Bruce and the others were waiting in a rental car out front. I got in the back seat and we took off.

"Everyone else is already there," said Lugo. "The rehearsal and other stuff."

"Thanks for calling me. I'm glad I was home."

I felt a little awkward because I hadn't seen Bruce since I had declined to co-sign his lease application, but he was nice and cordial and talked to me and wasn't mad at all. We drove south for an hour and then hit the Pacific Coast Highway and finally up a long, high hill to a chapel and grass area, a very romantic site indeed.

"Wow, this is nice," I said.

We got there right on time and soon the wedding started in the small chapel and there was maybe thirty people there, at most, and I knew a fair amount of them. I was one of about two white people because, heck, it was a Japanese affair with mostly Japanese people. Lugo was the only Hispanic person. I hung around him a lot because neither of us was accustomed to some of the Japanese customs. It was a short ceremony and it was nice and the day was perfect and cool and there were lots of pictures taken and I felt a part of something grand. An hour later everything had finished and I got a ride back to the hotel with the others.

"You sure you don't want to come to the reception?" asked Bruce once the car stopped.

"No, thanks. I promised Sakura I would take her out."

They knew about her because I had mentioned he a little during the drive.

"Okay, thanks for coming today."

"Thanks for inviting me."

A week later they prepared to leave again, this time to live in New York, and I knew I had made the right decision about not signing that lease.

"Are you guys coming back?"

"Maybe," said one of them. "Maybe not."

And it was a cryptic response and in my heart I wondered if I would see them again because they were going to New York and maybe it's a great place to live and stay but I knew I wouldn't live there. I loved L.A. too much, loved the hot summers and thick smog, loved the delicious variety of landscape and so many other things.

I watched them ride away in the cab and I wondered about them. I wished them the best and could only hope that I would see them again and that they would be safe and that good things would happen to them. Maybe I could have helped them stay in L.A., but I hadn't and that was that and they were gone and life went on for me and everyone else. A very long time would pass before I would see them again and then things would be different, a lot different, and they would be worse, a lot worse, and it would disturb me because I would feel responsible because I could have done something about it but I didn't. I didn't do what I should have done.

II

Having been rejected by Shizu, I deliberately tried to do great things with Sakura and made sure that Shizu found out about them, either directly from me or indirectly through Sakura or Harry. We would drive all around, to Malibu or Santa Monica, to the movies, out to eat, anywhere and everywhere.

One day I invited myself to Shizu's room when Harry wasn't around and I started talking to her and then all she could talk of was Harry and pretty soon it was obvious that she wanted me to leave, and this infuriated me even more.

I had a regular paycheck coming in from the job at the newspaper. I didn't like things there and recently they had taken a turn for the worse, but I had money coming in so Sakura and I went out often and went to the movies and ate at restaurants. I knew that she talked to Shizu regularly so I wanted to do as many fun things as possible, so that word of them would get back to Shizu and make her jealous, in part because I had a car, Harry didn't, and I could take Sakura all over town if we wanted to go.

One day we went to Beverly Hills and I showed her my old apartment there and then we hung out in Roxbury Park and chased each other in the enclosed lawn bowling area until we got chased out by the local park security, given the fact that that area was off limits to non-lawn bowlers.

We went to the Beverly Center and also to Century City Plaza and that shopping area. We went to the mall in Santa Monica, the one near Westwood, and ate at the same places I had eaten I when I had been there a year and a half earlier.

All of this activity with Sakura must have bothered Yasu in some way. Maybe he didn't like Sakura and didn't like the fact that I was dating her. Maybe he was still embarrassed over what had happened in her room that one night. Either way, he hardly ever called me and made a point of not going anywhere with me or doing anything if he knew that Sakura was coming too, and of course she often was because she was my girlfriend.

One day I got a call from Yasu and this surprised me but I figured he wanted a ride somewhere and of course I was right.

"Is there any way you can take me somewhere?" he asked. "I don't like the community college I'm at now and I want to transfer. There's one in Long Beach I like and also one in Seattle."

"Sure, no problem."

"Oh good, I appreciate it."

I figured it would be a nice drive and I had never been to the beach in Long Beach and I wanted to see it. So an hour later we left and I drove him down there and on the way he talked about wanting to transfer and not really knowing where he wanted to go, but he had narrowed it down to two schools. We got to the Long Beach Community College and Yasu and I walked around and got some brochures.

"I thought the city would be different here," he said.

"Yeah, it's a real industrial neighborhood. Look at those smoke stacks."

"It's not so nice."

"It's definitely not Beverly Hills."

"No, not at all."

After he had gotten his info and forms, I decided to drive over to the beach area. It was a nice sunny day and I wanted to relax a bit.

"I wouldn't go swimming here," I said once we were on the beach.

"Why?"

"Pollution. Look, there's not a single person in the water."

"No, I don't see anybody."

"Hey, I have an idea. Let's rent one of those carts there."

And that's what we did. We rented one of those four-wheel pedal-propelled carts for an hour and had a grand time pedaling up and down the sidewalk on the beach and this was the last time that Yasu and I had fun together, the very last time. We even crashed into the sound a couple times but that mad even more enjoyable.

Yasu and I had a great time this day and it was fun to get away and go to Long Beach thought realized quickly that it wasn't my favorite location, that I much preferred the beaches at Santa Monica or Venice or even Malibu.

I had a feeling that Yasu was serious about leaving and I didn't want him to go because I considered him my friend even though things had been different recently. And I wondered why I lived in a hotel building anyway, where by definition people didn't stay very long, where one shouldn't get attached to people who were but temporary residents.

12

I was still working at the paper, but I really wanted to be doing work in publishing, and the politics had work had gotten to me, what with all the lies by management and the telemarketing disguised as customer service, and everything else that I disliked.

So I saw an ad in the paper for an assistant editor at a psychology text publisher, so I applied for the position and submitted my resume. They granted me an interview and luckily they scheduled it on a Friday, a day I was off at the paper because I was on the Monday-through-Thursday, ten-hour-a-day schedule.

I got to their company, out in the valley somewhere, and was nearly late because there was construction and road repairs going on all over the place. I explained to the interviewer my background and my internships and my degree in psychology and everything else.

"This is just a preliminary interview," she said. "It's just to screen out unqualified applicants."

"Okay."

"We'll schedule second interviews later on for those who are qualified."

"Great."

The interview ended and I went back to the hotel and felt great about my chances for a second interview and a job. I figured I was a shoo-in because I had some journalism experience and a solid psychology background. This confidence made me think about quitting my job at the paper.

A week later things got really bad at the paper and I kept showing up late and finally the main supervisor called me in to talk to him during the start of a shift. I was sick of the boredom of cubicles, the endless calls, the lies and deceit, the way the employees were treated, and so many other things.

And the fact that I figured I would be hired at the publishing company made me arrogant and a real jerk and I blurted out every thing I hated about the company to this man.

"Maybe we don't have a position for you any more. Maybe it's not the best place for you."

"It's not."

Then things became tense in that small cramped space and I was close to yelling at him and cussing and throwing a fit. I bet he sensed this.

"You should leave now," he said.

"I am."

"Just make sure you put it in writing."

I walked out of his dumb office and headed back to my cubicle and as I did so I looked at all the familiar faces around me, I marveled at how fast the months had gone by, and I knew I was quitting yet another job. I picked out my personal belongings from my cubicle. I turned and saw the girl I had fallen for, the one who sat right behind me, and I knew I would miss her the most. I grabbed a pen and paper and scribbled a very brief resignation note and dropped it along with my room key card onto one of the supervisor's desks as I left, then immediately I wished I hadn't written it because I wouldn't be able to get unemployment compensation. But I figured I wouldn't need it because surely I would get the publishing position. That night I called my coworker, the guy with whom I had driven to work on so many days, and he told me that everyone had talked about me that day, of how they couldn't believe how angry I had seemed or why I quit so suddenly.

"Sorry I won't be able to give you any more rides," I said.

"Don;t worry about that. I'll be fine. I'm just worried about you."

"I've already got a better position lined up, in something I want to do."

"Good."

I hung up and realized that I wouldn't be going back to that paper ever again, and it kind of hit me hard.

Sure enough, the next day I got a call for them and they wanted to set me up for a second interview. I went to that one and they tested me on my editing skills and I did very poorly on it and tried to defend myself.

"I just need some practice, some training," I said.

"We could train anybody."

"I work hard."

"We're looking for someone with more experience and skills than you have."

Then, right then, I knew I wasn't going to get hired. I left and the drive back to the hotel took forever and now things were terrible because I didn't have a job and didn't have the potential for one at another company. And I couldn't see how things had come to that, how I kept repeating myself and quitting and messing up my life to the extreme.

13

Life went on at the hotel and David always complained about the mental hospital that he felt the hotel was, none of us liked the bad food in the cafeteria and hated the fact that we had to pay for it as part of the rent, and sometimes the bad neighborhood got to us because of all the police sirens and police helicopters.

"How's your book coming along?" said Dave to Jose one day when the three of us were down in the recreation room.

"I have one chapter," said Jose with a smile.

"You're writing a book?" I asked him.

"Trying to."

"That's cool." I wondered what his book was going to be about. "What else do you do all day?"

"I watch Charlie Rose. He had a great interview last night."

"Do you work?"

He shook his head no.

"Do you go to school?"

"I used to but dropped out. My parents still think I do and they'd be pretty angry if they knew the truth."

Jose was cool and I liked him a lot as a friend and thought that it was great that he was on some sort of permanent vacation.

"Harry wanted me to work on his movies, with dialogue, but I told him I was busy with my book."

"I don't mind helping him," I said, and I didn't.

That weekend Harry and I worked on "Dirty Laundry" some more and I asked him when we could film it, but he was noncommittal and simply said that he wanted that one to be great.

Instead, we worked on "Over the Edge," the third and last part of the story that began with "Trouble on the Home Front," and started filming it and I ended up being the main actor in it, though of course Jose and David and some others were in it too. It had a serious plot and story deficiency, and I couldn't do much to improve it because he had certain shots that he was adamant about keeping and so we had to work with that and do the best we could. The film started out on the roof where my character was about to jump off and I ran and ran with my briefcase and almost jumped off when I stopped and was reminded of something and then the flashbacks began. Harry put all the scenes together really well, too well actually because it was a lot to take in and comprehend, and edited everything and included a soundtrack and music that fit perfectly. Yasu was in this film as well as Dave, Jose, Rebecca and some others. It ended up being great and nearly won an award in one of his classes.

After he finished this we started the writing and idea phase of a new short film called "Shakedown 1999." We tossed ideas around and imagined what we could do with it and what it could be about. And our lives were like this, always talking about a film idea or working on one or setting up a scene or figuring out who could do what in a part and on and on, and I enjoyed it and he did too and everything was great as I worked with Harry on his films.

14

One day I called Rebecca and went to her room and hung around with her for a while, then we decided to go do some things together.

"How are your classes?" I asked Rebecca as we drove west on Wilshire Boulevard, on our way to the west side of L.A..

"Okay, but I have to do my film and I still don't have an idea what I can do it about."

"Lemme help you. You could do it on anything. I've got a zillion ideas."

"Like what?"

"Just look around. See that mailbox over there? You could do a story centered around a mailbox."

"That's silly."

"I'm serious. It could be like a character and you could have all these people who walk by it and have conversations near it and maybe someone sends off a package and the whole reason he's sending it off, or maybe there's a letter to a secret lover. There's all kinds of things you could do with it."

"I don't know."

"I'll help you. We can make it work. You know I can write all kinds of stories and it's way easy to make them happen near a mailbox. There's that one outside the hotel. You can shoot there and everybody we know can come down and be in a scene. It'll be great."

"All right."

"Great, now I'm excited. I'll start work on it tonight. You'll see, it'll work."

"Yeah, maybe."

And then later in the week I had a whole list of ideas for Rebecca's movie and so I called her and then went up to her room and told her about it all.

"You can call it Mailbox, Mailbox something," I said.

"Mr. Mad Mailbox?"

"Perfect. Here's what I've got." I gave her my notes. "Just take whatever you like best. It's your film so all of this is just some suggestions."

"Okay."

"You could start shooting in the morning and shoot throughout the day like it's a day in the life of a mailbox or something. And then some characters could appear and then reappear at a later time when something else happens."

"Right."

"Maybe it's just a series of short clips."

"Like that movie about thirty short stories about Glenn Gould."

"Exactly. But maybe some of yours have a story to them, just to make it interesting. Like one could be a bitter love triangle and we see the beginning in the morning and then, since you're not using dialogue, maybe it could be a lot of gestures and physical stuff, looking around so as not to get caught."

"Like the girlfriend finds out that the guy is seeing someone else."

"Yes."

"Maybe she saw him with the other girl, saw them go into the hotel, holding hands and being all affectionate."

"Right. So I've got that story you could center the other action around. Here's some ideas for the short, non-related clips. One could be just a boy riding his bike and, you know, he comes around the corner too fast and crashes into the mailbox and falls down and then limps off injured."

"That would be funny."

"And maybe something where someone stops by and can't find the mail slot, and just drops of the letter on top and it blows away. And you know how some people drop in their mail one letter at a time and take forever and forever doing so?"

"Yeah."

"You could have one guy put in his letters like that and there's this guy, I think Jose would be perfect for this, and he's really impatient and he has to watch the slow guy go through all this and then Jose gets really mad and does something, like they get in a fight or something crazy. Jose was perfect at this when we did that 'Out of Focus' short film."

"I saw that," said Rebecca. "He was hilarious."

"So we have to get him to be in it. And maybe Yasu could so something and everybody else and have all kinds of characters and interesting situations. You can look over this list and tell me what you want to do and I'll help out with whatever you need."

"I've gotta get it done really fast because of how long it takes to get it developed and I still have to add music to it."

"We could do it on Saturday. Can you get the film you need by then?"

"Yeah, I might have enough already."

"I'm not doing anything on Saturday. Let's do it then."

"I don't know. There seems to be so much to do. I don't want it to end up like the film I did on the beach."

"It won't be like that. It'll be lots of fun and I'll help you out a lot. We can get it done."

"I don't know, maybe."

It was so frustrating to me how Rebecca was, how she couldn't make a decision sometimes, how it seemed so hard for her to know what to do. I was excited and maybe I had the personality temperament of liking to get things done and to just grab a camera and start shooting. But Rebecca wasn't like this and neither was Harry and it just killed me because it seemed to take forever to get them going. But that was how it was and I was just the writer. All I could do was offer my help and leave it to Rebecca to decide if and when she wanted to do her film. It was her project after all. I said goodbye and went back to my room.

15

I found work again. A major department store was hiring for holiday work and so of course I thought that was perfect because I could work in the evenings and then keep looking for a real job in the daytime and interview in the mornings or afternoons. But this job only lasted one night and that was because there was a severe lack of training in he company and they just set me out on the floor one evening in housewares and told me to start working and I didn't know how to do anything and just walked away form all that mess. They actually wanted to train me after I started working.

I went back to the hotel and Yasu was amazed when I told him that I quit.

"What?" he exclaimed. "You just started."

"I know. It was too awful."

"You need to give it a chance."

"I don't need it. I'll get a good job soon."

We talked some more and hung out but he didn't seem interested and had maybe grown tired of me, so I excused myself and went back to my room. I hardly saw Yasu after this. I heard, maybe from Harry or possibly Rebecca, that Yasu was going to move out, though I thought for sure he would stay and go to the community college in Long Beach. I called him up to verify this.

"Yeah, I've decided to go to Seattle," he said.

"Isn't that where your sister lives?"

"Yeah. She doesn't want me to go there but I think it's best for me."

Now I personally didn't see the logic in this because there were plenty other community colleges in California and Oregon and even Washington to which he could have transferred. The one in Seattle, from what I had read about it, was not particularly better than any of those in California, and not less expensive either.

"When are you going?" I asked.

"Saturday afternoon."

"Well, maybe we could go out for breakfast in the morning before you leave."

"Okay, yes."

"I'll call you then."

I hung up and realized that my relationship with him had deteriorated a great deal since he and Shizu had interrupted me and Sakura that one night, and I knew this was because, for whatever reason, Yasu disliked Sakura a lot. Maybe it was because I spent a lot less time with Yasu when I started dating Sakura. Maybe Yasu didn't like this and took a disliking to Sakura because of it. I certainly don't remember him being hostile to her in any way before we started being together.

"I'm sorry that you're leaving," I said on Saturday morning after Yasu and I had ordered our breakfast at Denny's. "But it's probably good for you. Any place besides Koreatown is an improvement."

"They have a much better program in Seattle."

"And I hear there's a big Japanese and Asian population up there. That's gotta be a good thing for you. I've been there once before and you've gotta go to the downtown market. It's right by the port and they have this thing where they throw fish."

"What?"

"Like in the commercials. Well, you'll see. Everybody knows about it."

"Okay. My sister isn't too happy about it. She told me not to come, to go somewhere else."

"Oh I bet. I mean, of all the cities in the U.S., you're moving to the one where she lives."

"It's the school there. That's why I picked Seattle."

"Right." I said this and nodded my head and tried to give the impression that I believed him, though I didn't at all. Even if it was true, he should have had the decency to stay out of where his sister lived anyway. It was inconsiderate and impolite of him to pick the one city in the U.S. where his sister lived and went to school. But maybe I was still mad at him for how he had changed so suddenly once he found out that I was involved with Sakura. I guess it could all be traced back to that one night when Yasu and Shizu were worried about Sakura and they forced themselves into her room when I was there. It was his behavior then that gave it all away and it just killed me how he had acted, like he was all embarrassed because of what surely had been going on between me and Sakura during that time. Even better, Shizu was quite nonchalant about it and didn't make a big deal about it at all and that was just great to me, that she would be so sensitive and considerate about the whole thing. But maybe I still had feelings for her and I know I did and couldn't for the life of me figure out what she saw in Harry.

"I guess you'll be leaving from LAX tonight," I said. "You know, I used to work there and I miss it sometimes. I know where all the plane terminals are located."

"That's right, that's the airport."

"You gonna call a taxi? Make sure they don't cheat you because I know they do sometimes. Make'em give you a fare estimate right away."

"Yes."

I knew what I was doing. I knew that he didn't want to have to spend money on a taxi because it would be expensive. I was enjoying myself in this behavior and I thought it was fair of me to do so, given how he had acted toward me recently, and maybe I wouldn't have been doing that if he hadn't been so obvious in his dramatic change of friendship. There's nothing I hate more than people who betray me, who are my friend one day but then when something happens they change and they really weren't my friend after all. As I sat there and ate my French fries I thought of all the times when I wanted to go somewhere and I offered him the chance to come with me but he declined the second after I mentioned that Sakura also would be coming with us. What kind of a person is that, I ask you, who predicates his friendship with conditions. Not much of one.

"You know, the light rail subway system goes real close to the airport. I guess it's not really a subway after it leaves the downtown area because then it's above ground and becomes like a train. But I know you can take it south really far and then take it west and it goes within, I think, maybe a mile of the airport. Pretty good for the price but then that's a lot of luggage." I ate and watched Yasu and knew exactly what he was thinking and knew that he knew that I had a car and that I could easily take him to the airport.

"Do you think you could drive me to the airport?" he asked finally.

I enjoyed the moment. I got what I wanted and that was him having to humble himself and actually have to ask something from me and it must have been hard because both of us knew that he had treated me differently recently and I had every reason to say no because, honestly, I couldn't care less about him any more and was glad that he was leaving.

"Sure, I can give you a ride."

"Thank you, thanks so much."

"Of course, it'll be fun."

We ate the rest of our breakfast and walked back to the hotel. He was ready a few hours later and called me. I brought my car out in front of the hotel, a step away from the big awning out front, and Yasu came out with his luggage.

"Did you check out?" I asked.

"Oh yes, about an hour ago."

"Then we're off." I drove him south and then we got on the Santa Monica Freeway and made our way west and then got on the 405 and soon we got to the airport and found his terminal. "Here we are." I helped him with us luggage and we shook hands. "Hope to see you again," I lied.

"You too. Thanks for everything."

I had a feeling that he was sorry about some things, based on the way he was acting, and suddenly I felt sorry for him and regretted the fact that he was moving away.

"Make sure you keep in touch," I said with a smile. "We sure had a lot of fun together. Maybe you could come back and work on a sequel to one of Harry's movies."

"Yes, I'd like that."

"Good luck." And then he walked away and I got in my car and headed home and I thought I would never see him again. And I was really ambivalent about everything that had happened between us.

A week later I got postcard from Yasu and he mentioned how he was enjoying his new life with his host family and he really liked his school and Seattle was wonderful and he hoped everyone was doing well. And I heard that he called Jose and David a few times but he didn't call me at all and then I hated him after that because nothing had changed and he was now a jerk and I hoped to god that he never called me because if he did, well, I would just hang up real fast. I was glad he was out of my life, glad that he had gone to another city in a state far way. My, how things had changed between us. I thought back to when we first met and how he just wanted me to help him learn more English and how we hadn't done that at all but had just had lots of fun at the movies and beaches and all over town. I don't think I taught him one thing about the English language, but surely we taught each other a few things about loyalty or the lack thereof.

16

I searched all over for work and applied in greater Los Angeles and in the valley for anything for which I was qualified or anything I found even the slightest bit interesting in the field of media or publishing or journalism. Finally, one Sunday I saw an ad for an open house recruiting session for a major cable company in town. They advertised that they were looking to hire a hundred positions and I knew that this was my chance. I got dressed the next day and drove up to Hollywood and found the building. I went inside through the west entrance.

"I'm here for the open house," I said.

"That's on the other side of the building. You'll see the sign."

"Thanks." On my way out I saw some flyers listing all of the hundreds of channels and specials and packages that were available from this company. There were pictures and images of popular movies and popular movie stars and everything looked wonderful and I felt good because I lived in L.A. and I would be working for another media company again. I just knew that my chances of getting work at this company had to be great.

I walked around and found an entrance through a gate and then found the main entrance and went inside. There was a very large room with lots of tables and dozens and dozens of people, maybe even a hundred total in fact, sitting at the tables and filling out applications. I followed suit and sat at one of the remaining open spots, in the middle of a table in the center of the room.

I had all the information from my other jobs with me as well as my resume so I started filling out the application. Every once in a while I looked up and saw someone finish their application and take it to one of the employees or supervisors who were sitting at tables against the walls. I filled mine out very fast because I had done it so much recently, filled out so many applications all over town, so much that I knew all the addresses and phone numbers of my other employers by heart.

This was the same company with which I had been affiliated when I was in Stockton, when I had volunteered as a camera operator for the cable access channel, and so I put this down in the section on the application for additional information. I knew that the position for which they were hiring was in customer service, over the phone in fact, and so I exaggerated on what I had done at my other jobs, and emphasized the similarities between my former responsibilities and this opening. Soon I finished, got up, and took my application over to a supervisor.

"I'm finished," I said. "Am I supposed to do something next?"

"Just have a seat. We're doing interviews in the other room so it'll be a little while before we get to you."

"Okay."

I went back to where I had been sitting and waited. This was exciting for me because I figured my chances in my head for the job and I was confident that applying on the first of the two days of the open house was better than applying on the second day. I sat up straight, fixed my tie, and watched the other people around me. After ten minutes I watched as a man from one of the supervisor tables got up and walked over to me.

"Sorry to keep you waiting," he whispered softly. "We'll try and get you in right away."

"All right," I said back. He went back to his table and I tried not to look in his direction. I wondered why he had even bothered telling me this because I didn't mind waiting. I certainly had nothing else to do or nowhere else to go. Then I looked around the giant room, glanced up and down all of the tables in the room, and I realized why the white man had spoken to me. Hard as it was for me to believe, I was the only white applicant in the room at that moment. There had to be at least a hundred people sitting at all of the benches and I had looked at all of them. Most of the applicants were black and the rest, except me, were Asian. I couldn't believe it. This was my first experience being a minority in a room, a minority in the loosest definition of the term, and I felt what the man had said to me had been wrong. It was discrimination and racism but in the reverse. I was getting preferential treatment, or at least the suggestion of it, and this bothered me because it wasn't fair to the others. I despised the man. I despised that he had said what he had said to me. I should not be given preferential treatment, or any different type of treatment, because of the color of my skin. The whole thing made me sick.

I waited some more and soon my name was called and I was taken to a back room. I almost, but didn't, request that the woman make sure that I wasn't going ahead of anybody else. That wouldn't have been right, but I needed a job and I wasn't going to do anything to jeopardize it.

"Hello," I said after I was greeted by an employee and taken to a desk area where someone would interview me.

"Good morning," said the woman. "Hope it didn't take too long to get in here."

"Not at all." I decided against telling her how I had been singled out, in a minor way, and that I was probably being interviewed sooner than other people who had finished their applications before me.

"I have your resume here, but why don't you tell me a little about you."

"Okay, well I've actually worked for this company before, well volunteered really. I was a camera operator for the branch up in Stockton and I did my best to get a comedy show at the cable access channel, though it never worked out. Here's a reference from the station manger there." I gave it to her and continued. "I've done other media work, like in newspapers and magazines, but now I'm interested in the programming side." This was an outright lie but it didn't matter.

"This is a good place to start," she said. "And then she asked me some standard questions and then I gave her a reference letter from when I was a volunteer photographer for a film commission up in San Joaquin County.

"All right, everything looks good," she said. "We'll be calling people soon and then there'll be training that lasts a month. You'll also be required to get a physical and a TB test and they'll have to be done before you can begin at the main office, but you can train while you get it done. Training happens at a different location."

"No problem. I hope I get the job."

I shook her hand and then left the company and felt that I had a real good chance at the job, and this time I promised that I wouldn't quit like all the other jobs, no matter what the scenario was or how things worked out. I hated quitting jobs and having to start all over somewhere else.

17

As I waited to hear about the job, I continued to try and have fun and do things, though I was strapped for cash most of the time. There was no shortage of things to see and do nearby. There were always movies being filmed in the area near the hotel, often at the hotel across the street or in some of the nearby parking lots. And one night there were big scenes shot in the street and rain machines were used to make rain and everyone was fascinated by it except me. I was bored by it most of all. One time there was a movie made in the lobby of the hotel, and when I walked out on the way to work I had to walk around all these cameras, lights, actors, wires, microphones, and other movie equipment, and I remember being irritated by how they took up the whole lobby of the hotel. I liked it most when I was either making movies with Harry or anybody else, or when I was going to the movies with someone.

There were always free movie passes available. I got some to "The English Patient" by writing to a TV station when they were having a promotion. Rebecca and I went to see that picture and we had a great time and really were impressed by the picture. I went with Sakura to see a sneak preview of "Ransom" with Mel Gibson. Dave and I went for free to "Blood and Wine" with Jack Nicholson. And Harry, Shizu and I went to the world premiere of "McHale's Navy," though we regretted doing so afterwards. And best of all, though we weren't able to get free tickets,

Sakura and I went to see a special screening of "The Big Sleep," and when it was over I classified it as my favorite film ever because of the rich, witty dialogue, the tough-guy character played by Bogart, and the sensual, insolent character played by Bacall.

Still, I needed money for my bills and for rent and gas and still hadn't heard about the cable company job. Luckily, my family came down to go to Disneyland and they invited me and said they would pay for anything so of course I went and had a grand time. But my rent was due that day and that was all I could think of and the fact that I didn't have enough money to pay it, but I asked my parents to lend me some money and of course they helped me out. And at the end of the day at Disneyland, I drove from Anaheim back to the hotel and was able to pay my rent for December and felt a whole lot better. Then I went straight to Sakura's room and gave her a small Disney figurine I had purchased for her and she liked it a lot and thanked me and all was well.

I was hanging out with Dave and Jose in the lobby the next night when Sakura walked by to use the pay phones.

"There goes your girlfriend," said David.

"She's not my girlfriend," I said, though I wasn't sure why I said it, except maybe that I wanted my girlfriend to be someone else.

"Just like Harry and Shizu."

And then I knew why I denied involvement with Sakura, because I didn't want to be like Harry, not in any way at all. Except that I did want his girlfriend Shizu and always thought of a way I could get her to think well of me.

After using the phone Sakura glared at me on the way out and I knew she was still mad at me because the day before I had yelled at her a few times in my room and screamed at her to leave me alone and to get out of my room and stay out and stop asking to stay the night in my room. Now I can't recall why I had done that, though I could relate it to the stress in my life due to my financial situation, but this would just be an excuse and a terrible one at that. I guess a lot of the reason why I treated her poorly was because I was really in love with Shizu and she didn't like me back and that's terribly frustrating.

Soon Sakura moved out to an apartment building nearby and that actually improved things between us. I called her a lot and went to visit her there and she was very happy to be out of the hotel and glad that she had friends she could live with, a pretty Japanese girl and her boyfriend, though she said that she didn't get along with the boyfriend because he never paid for anything and freeloaded off Sakura's friend. I was glad to get out of the hotel to visit Sakura at her place and we had lots of great time sin her room. One day I picked up a complimentary poster from work. These things were free because of the industry in which we worked. And it was a Brad Pitt poster and I knew how much Sakura liked Brad Pitt. I stopped by her place but she was with some friends.

"I won't stay," I said. "I just wanted to give you this poster."

"Thank you so much," she said when she looked at it.

I left and went back to the hotel and let her socialize with her new friends, and I was glad that she had new friends and didn't have to talk to Shizu any more. But the fact that Sakura no longer stayed at the hotel meant that I had more time to talk to Shizu and hang out with her in any context I could think of.

I thought of Shizu a lot and wanted to do things with her and one night I was able to convince her and Yasu to go with me to see the Christmas lights in a big forest area nearby, but I got lost for nearly an hour and was lucky I found the place at all.

18

I got a call and was offered the job at the cable company and I felt great because I was really getting worried about my financial situation and I needed cash pretty badly. I had paid my rent for December but had almost no money to live on after that, except for some credit on my charge cards.

I was told where to go for training and when I got there they gave us all explicit instructions on the hours of the training, that we would get paid for the training at a rate just slightly than our salary was going to be, and that we would be paid the first time right before Christmas, and of course this made everyone, especially me, very happy.

So I started the customer service training with everyone else and we learned all about the channels and packages that people purchased and how much they cost and what pay-per-view was and how that worked and lots of other things. The training wasn't bad except that I felt a little awkward at times because it was pretty obvious that I was in the minority given the high percentage and black or African-American employees in the employ of the company. I didn't mind this and hardly noticed it at all because I'm a fairly friendly and talkative person and get along with most everybody and I couldn't care less where they come from or what color they are just so long as they're nice to me and talk back to me when I talk to them.

On one day during this training I was sent out with a cable installer guy, the person who hooks up cable boxes for people or rewires the cable lines when they go out. And we went all over the city and to all kinds of different places and of course there were some people who tried to bribe him into giving them free cable, but the guy just couldn't do it because everything was computerized now and he had no control over the channels because it was all done by computer at the main location.

I kept training at the cable company and they reminded all of us to make sure we got our physicals and TB tests, which they agreed to pay for, because we wouldn't be allowed to start work at the main office until we did. So I drove down to the appointed facility in some industrial town and had it all done and was given a TB shot and was told that if there was a reaction and if it didn't go away for a few days, then I probably had TB, but they would do an x-ray to confirm it of course.

So I went home and watched my arm and waited a couple days and there was an obvious reaction because it started to swell and I got really nervous and called them and made an appointment for an x-ray as soon as was possible. I figured that I probably got TB from living in Koreatown or maybe from living in the old hotel building. I had no idea how I had contracted but I figured that I had and so I became a bit distressed and depressed for a while, but maybe some of that had to do that I didn't have any money, because I quit the newspaper job.

"I've decided that I'm going to dye my hair," I said to Rebecca one night. "It's gonna be pitch black. Can you help me do it?"

"Okay. You sure you want to do it?"

"Yes."

"Maybe I'll do mine at the same time."

Now Rebecca already had nice hair, it was a lovely dark brown, so I couldn't see why she wanted to dye hers, but I was happy to have her join me and so we bought the supplies and went to my room and dyed her hair and mine and helped each other and it was a fun and interesting night.

"Actually, I think I might have some rare and incurable disease," I admitted. "So black really matches my mood."

"What is it, lime disease?"

"No, TB. But I have an appointment for an x-ray tomorrow so I'll know for sure then."

"Maybe I shouldn't hang out with you. Is it contagious?"

"I probably don't have it. Last year I got vaccinated for it so the antibodies are probably in my system and that's why I get a reaction."

"So why are you doing this to your hair?"

"Any reason is good enough."

"Okay."

"Hey, the cable company is throwing this big party and gambling night later in the month. Would you like to go?"

"Yeah, sure."

"It's semi-formal so we'll have to dress nice."

"That's fine. We can go shopping."

"Okay, then it's set. I'll let you know the details."

I had the x-ray taken later and of course it came back negative and I felt better but didn't regret having dyed my hair.

19

A week passed and soon it was the day of the gambling party get-together for the employees at the cable company, including me of course. I had gotten my two passes from work and told everyone there that I would take all their chips at the tables. They had told us that we would be able to get chips by cashing in the money coupons we received at the door, then if we wanted we could cash in our chips at the end of the night for prizes.

I called Rebecca that Saturday morning.

"Hey, you still want to go to the event tonight?"

"Yes, but I don't have anything fancy to wear."

"I don't think it matters that much."

"Can we still go shopping?"

"Sure," I said. "How about the Beverly Center? There's plenty of clothing shops there."

"All right."

"I've gotta do some things this morning. You wanna leave at two? That should give us plenty of time to shop and then come back here and change. The thing doesn't really start until eight."

"What's going to happen there?"

"I'm not sure. There's the dinner which is supposed to be catered and then we just hang out and gamble for the rest of the night, for as long as we want."

"Sounds good. I'll be in my apartment after noon."

"Okay." I hung up. I had promised that I would do something with Sakura that day so I walked down the street and to the other side of Wilshire. I loved her new place and loved her room there and the fact that she had so much privacy and we could both be away from everyone at the hotel. We went out to lunch and I spent the last of my money but it was great spending time with her again.

"I have to do some things for the rest of the day," I said. "Will you be home tomorrow?"

"Maybe, maybe not. I might go to the beach with my roommate."

"After how they treat you?"

"Sometimes people treat me mean but I still talk to them and do things with them."

I had a feeling, by the way she said this and looked at me, that she was referring to me and some of my past actions. Her point was well taken by me and I knew I had been in the wrong before.

"I'll call you first," I said. I went back to the hotel and went straight to Rebecca's room and soon we left for our shopping.

"I've got a better place in mind," I said. "Let's go to that shopping center in Century City."

"Fine by me."

We got there and it was fairly busy and soon she wanted to stop and get something to eat at one of the restaurants.

"I don't have any money," I said.

"But I don't want to eat alone."

"It's okay, I don't mind."

"But I do mind. It's awkward."

So I lied and said I would buy something and then after she bought something I went and joined her, though in fact I hadn't purchased anything at all.

"You said you were going to buy something," she said.

"I changed my mind."

"Don't do that."

And then it got much worse as she said some things and erupted in anger and I didn't know what to do so soon neither of us were talking to each other and it was terribly uncomfortable and awkward and I despised being near her. Finally she finished eating and the whole mess was over.

"Let's go shopping," I said.

We walked around to some shops and Rebecca looked at clothes.

"I think I'll go next door," she said.

We went outside and I saw an empty bench in front of the store.

"I'll go sit there and wait for you."

"Okay, I won't be long."

So I sat there and lots of people walked in front of me as I waited for Rebecca, and waited and waited. I looked at my watch and couldn't believe how long she was taking. Then I started to get angry because of this and what had happened an hour later at the restaurant. Then I grew more impatient and went inside the store to look for her but she wasn't there so I walked out and up and down the walking area. I waited some more for her in front of the store and then got really mad and irate and wondered if she had just took off. I figured she must have walked to my car, which I had parked near Roxbury Park, so I made my way out there but she wasn't there either. I waited and wondered what to do next and knew I couldn't leave her. So I headed back and finally saw her coming down the sidewalk on the way toward me. I was absolutely infuriated by this point and knew I had to calm down.

"Where have you been?" I asked, after taking a few breaths.

"Where were you? You said you'd wait outside the store at the bench."

"I did, for like forever, and you never came out."

"I did come back. I looked right at you and pointed to the store nearby. That was where I went."

"I didn't see you."

"I looked at you."

"Let's go."

I didn't say a word to her and we both got in my car and I took off. After two blocks I pulled over and stopped.

"I'm sorry for getting angry," I said. "What did you buy?"

"Okay. It took me a while to find it, but I like it."

I decided not to comment on exactly how long it took her.

"It was expensive," she said. She lifted it out of the bag and it was a really nice, cool-blue pullover shirt, but of an expensive variety. At first it looked too casual but upon further examination it was obviously meant to be worn to a nice affair.

"Very nice," I said.

"You like it?"

"I like it a lot." And indeed I did.

Rebecca and I were able to speak friendly to each other as I drove home. I thanked her for the day and went to my room and was glad to be away from her. I had almost said some things to her that I surely would have regretted. There was no way in hell I was going to go with her anywhere again, especially nowhere that night.

I took a shower and stretched out on my bed and took a nap. When I woke it was early evening so I just watched some television and relaxed. A little before eight I heard a loud pounding on my door.

I opened it and Rebecca was standing there.

"I almost forgot about the party. You still wanna go?"

"Of course," I lied. "Can you be ready soon?"

"Yes, meet me in my room."

I shut my door and changed my mind and decided that I would go after all. I wanted to see what Rebecca's shirt looked like on her and maybe the gambling would be fun.

I went to her room ten minutes later and we were on the freeway at a little past eight. We got to the hotel which was located in a rough city close to the airport. Rebecca looked very nice in her new shirt and I guess I can open now that I found her very attractive that night and both of us seemed to match, in that we both had black hair and blue shirts on. I liked Rebecca immensely on this evening.

The dinner was very nice and was served in a large dining hall with low lighting and fancy candles on the table. The food was delicious and I enjoyed this part of the evening. Soon it became obvious that most of the people at this party or reception were black, but that didn't matter to us because everyone was friendly and having fun and that's all that matters. After we ate we got some more drinks and walked around. I introduced Rebecca to some of my co-workers.

"Is this your wife?" asked one of my supervisors.

"No, we're friends," I said.

"You look like a couple, with your hair and shirts."

"We fight like a couple too," said Rebecca, and this made me and the people around me laugh, because it was so true and so honest. She said this and it was perfect and I loved her for it.

I went and gambled some and then gave all my winnings away after I couldn't lose it and kept doubling my money. Then Rebecca and I went home and I thanked her a lot for going with me, and when I went back to my room I knew that I cared for Rebecca immensely and sincerely hoped that she would always be a part of my life, even into the distant future.

I didn't have much cash so I decided to buy gifts for my family at Sears because that was the only credit card I had that had credit on it. I bought a bunch of stuff from there and then two days later I got the idea that I could buy jewelry from there and take it to a pawn shop and get cash for it.

So I bought an expensive gold necklace that was supposedly on sale at half price and took it to a pawn shop in Koreatown. It cost me over four hundred dollars on my card but I figured it might be worth it if I could get half that from the pawn man.

"How much for this?" I asked the man as I handed it under the bullet-proof glass to him.

He held it and examined it as I figured out the lowest price I would take.

"Twenty bucks," he said flatly.

"What?" I exclaimed dumbfoundedly. "How?"

"Everything in gold is weight. This necklace is light as air."

I was stunned. Maybe I could take it to another shop but I figured he was right about the value of it because, hell, I had bought the thing from Sears and Sears isn't known for its jewelry.

I went back to my apartment and happened to see Rebecca.

"Are you doing anything tomorrow?" she asked me.

"I'm going shopping."

"Great. Can I come? I want to get some gifts and send them home."

"Sure."

I followed her to her room and hung out with her and relayed the whole story of mine about the pawn shop idea and how desperate I was and how the idea didn't work and how I'd have to return the necklace the next day and have the charge removed.

"That's so funny, so interesting," she said. "It really is."

"Maybe, but it's not fun."

"Oh no, but that's so cool, that you would think to do that. Can I see the necklace?"

I showed it to her and then felt so down that I went to my room and just sat in the darkness for a while and wondered what had become of me and why I was so low on money and I knew it was because I quit my job and shouldn't have and now I was spaying for it in a big way.

A week later Rebecca stopped by to tell me that she was leaving.

"I'm going home first," she said. "And then to Aspen for some skiing and who knows where after that."

"But you'll be back?"

"Of course. I have my classes at the community college."

"Okay. Please keep in touch. I'll write to you."

"And I'll write back."

"Let me drive you to the airport."

"I was going to ask you to do that."

"I thought so, but I didn't want you to have to ask. Need help with your bags?"

"Yes, please."

I went and helped her and drove her to the airport and gave her a great big hug and wished her well.

"I'll miss you a lot. Come back soon," I said.

"I will. You take care."

And then Rebecca left and I went back to the hotel and it wasn't the same without her, especially given what we had been through recently. I missed her already and hoped for her quick and safe return.

20

Soon it was December and I was completely bored with the job at the cable company and wondered why I had accepted the position in the first place, but then I remembered why when I got my first check ad was able to pay some bills. Still, I always checked the Sunday classified ads in the hope that I would find something better or more interesting.

On Sunday I saw an ad for work at canneries in Alaska for the upcoming winter season there. I thought that would be exciting so I thought whether or not I could move out and leave town and do that, but the logistics of everything and the fact that I liked Sakura and liked my other friends made me decide against it. Though all week I thought of going to the open interview and recruiting session on the Friday and then I didn't go and regretted not going the day afterward because I least I could have gotten some information about it or a phone number that I could have used in the future.

I saw an ad for a job at a big media and advertising company on Sunset Boulevard, with pay starting higher than what I was making at the cable company, so of course I mailed and faxed my resume to the company along with a cover letter explaining my great interest in the position of Media Buyer Assistant. And I waited for a week and didn't hear anything back from them and so I figured they had hired someone else or that I just wasn't qualified.

Then there was a big advertisement for the Air Force and they were accepting new recruits and people interested in becoming an officer. So of course I jumped at this opportunity because it seemed so worthwhile. I called up their office and went over to Santa Monica and talked to the recruiter there and they set me up to take the officer test. I gathered all the paperwork that I needed to complete and was thrilled when I passed the test and was given the green light to begin the application. There was a five-year commitment and this bothered me a lot, but I started filling out the application and took my time on it as my life went on and I continued to work at the cable company.

Before I went home to be with my family for Christmas, I was called for an interview at a big media company, the one I had faxed and mailed my resume to three weeks before and had nearly forgotten about. The interview went well, or at least seemed to, and I was comforted by this chance at the job.

By this time at the hotel, most of the residents had left for the holidays and the place seemed empty. At least half of the people who lived there were students so it was no surprise that there was a significant drop in people around there. Harry, Jose, David, Rebecca, Sylvia, Yasu, Shizu, and Sakura had all left, some for up to a month, and I felt alone again and hated the feeling.

Early on Christmas morning I drove to the airport and parked in the temporary parking lot and then used the airplane ticket my mother had sent me and flew home for the day. When I got to the Sacramento airport, my parents didn't recognize me until I walked right up to them.

"What happened to your hair?" asked my dad.

"It's black," said my mom. "I looked at you but looked away because I knew it couldn't have been you."

"Oh, I dyed it," I explained as we headed to Stockton. "Wait, I almost forgot. I have to pick up one of my bags."

We went to the baggage retrieval area and waited until I found the gift that was for my mother. It was in a box and wrapped in colorful paper.

"They wouldn't let me take it on the plane," I said to my mother. "You'll see why when you open it."

"Why did you dye your hair?" asked my mom.

"I thought I was going to die. I had a TB test and it looked positive and so I dyed my hair in a state of mourning."

"Did you get an x-ray?"

"Yeah, it turned up negative."

"The reaction you get was just because you've had shots recently for it."

"Yeah, I found that out."

We made it home and had a nice Christmas and a wonderful meal and in the afternoon I helped my dad out front as we worked on the walkway that led from the gate to the porch. There was a big crack in it that had been there for ten years and we had never gotten around to repairing it.

"How do you want to fix this?" I asked.

"We'll have to break apart the section and pour some new concrete."

"We could just pour in a little in the crack."

"No, a quick fix isn't the best way for this project. Besides, we've got all afternoon."

We gathered the wheelbarrow and cement and sledge hammer and started work on the project. While we did this, my mother used the gardening tools I had given her as a gift.

"I see why they wouldn't let them on the plane," she said. "These could be used as weapons."

I started pounding away on the concrete and watched it crack after every blow.

"I'm thinking of joining the Air Force," I said. "I passed the officer exam."

"Is that what you want to do?"

"I don't know. It looks exciting and might provide some stability for me."

"You sure you're not just trying to escape some other things?"

"What do you mean?"

"Sometimes people join the military to escape from things in their life, and they think that getting into the army or whatever will make things better."

I thought about this as I used the sledge hammer and pounded away on the concrete and broke it into pieces so we could take it out.

"I've always wanted to join the military. Maybe this is my chance."

"Could be. It's your decision."

And as we talked more about it, as I broke the concrete pieces into smaller ones, I slowly began to realize what he meant and I discovered that I was interested in the Air Force for the wrong reasons, not because I loved the idea of being a navigator but because liked the idea of getting out of Koreatown.

By the time my father and I mixed a bag of concrete and poured it into the space where the broken section used to be, my steadfast commitment to joining the military had been broken apart. My father's suggestions and comments had been effective and now I knew I wasn't going to go after all. I discovered the crack in my own foundation and it was my desperation for a quick fix to my life situation down in L.A.

"Looks good," said my father after we finished. "Thanks for the help today."

"No, thank you. I'm not gonna go into the Air Force."

"It's a tough decision."

"It's the right thing to do."

We went inside, cleaned up, and had a nice Christmas dinner. Later that evening my parents took me back to the airport and I flew home. And it was a good thing that I had talked to him about how I was thinking about joining the military and it was an even better thing that he helped me see the truth about myself, that I needed to be stronger and face the facts of my own life and not just run off when things weren't going well for me. I needed to be stronger and I needed to face the hard times and get through them and know that if I was patient, if I was committed, then things would get better for me in due time. I just needed to wait and see and watch my life unfold and not be in a rush and not want things to happen sooner than they were supposed to happen. I needed to change but that wasn't going to happen and I knew it.

PART 3

A New Year and a New Job

I

The flight back into L.A. was wonderful because it was late in the evening and the metropolitan area was blazing in light and it was a splendid sight as I looked out of the airplane window. It was a better sight than that one night when there was so much smog and fog in the area that the city lights reflected off that canopy and it seemed nearly as bright as daylight. This happened quite a lot, the smog staying in the vicinity, and only on rare days did the Santa Ana winds blow it all away so that you could actually see the mountains.

I made it to the airport and couldn't help but reminisce about the time when I worked there as a skycap, way back in 1995. I left the terminal and walked around the airport more than I had to because of how much I wanted to think back to those times and how far away they seemed, though it had only been two years. I heard the same recorded messages about the different lanes within the airport, the white ones for certain vehicles, the yellow ones for taxis, the red lanes for emergency vehicles and blue ones for handicapped. And I saw the taxis lined up at each station, the numbers of which called out to me as I passed and I simply shook my head and moved on.

Finally I found my car in one of the parking areas. I couldn't believe that I had left earlier that morning and now I was right back in the city, much like when I had flown from Reno to L.A. for the interview for the internship at Premiere. I had the bit of money my parents had given me for Christmas and I needed it when I paid my parking fee. It was a lot more than I thought it would be and it killed me to have to pay it because I knew that my rent was due soon and I wasn't going to have enough money for it. My parents had given me a decent amount of cash and I hadn't had the heart to tell them that I was in dire straights and needed a heck of a lot more. I certainly didn't want to let on that I was desperate. Actually, I had lied to them and said that I was still working at the paper even though I had quit in early November. I didn't want them to think that I wasn't responsible and I didn't want them to think that I couldn't take care of myself. I wasn't going to let on that I didn't know what I was doing half the time. Really, I shouldn't have quit that newspaper job without having something else lined up for sure. I know that I thought I had a good chance at that job in the valley at the psychological text-editing service but I didn't get it and then I had nothing. I guess I do that a lot, quit jobs because I think something else is coming. I told myself not to do it again.

I drove through the city on my way back to the apartment building in Koreatown and had a great, enjoyable time along the way. I had been gone for less than a day but it seemed longer for some reason. It was good to get away and even better to return and I wondered why I wanted to leave at all when L.A. was so much fun and so diverse and so big and thrilling and there was always something to do even when I didn't have any money. I liked where I lived and I liked my friends there. I liked the fact that people came there from all parts of the world and I never knew who would show up next. It was exciting. Going home to Stockton had helped me a lot because it got that whole air force idea out of my head. Although it did sound exciting, the prospect of joining the military, I knew I wasn't any good at making commitments and a five-year commitment was an impossibility for me for sure. Five months seemed a lifetime, let alone five years, and it was hard for me to keep the same job for that long. Five years could never happen. No way at all.

When I got back to my room, I counted the money I had in the bank and realized that I didn't have enough money for rent which was due in a week. I wasn't sure what to do. I didn't want to leave and I didn't have any credit available on my charge cards. I had had an interview at the media company before Christmas but they hadn't called me back yet. But I had to do something and so I went downstairs to talk to the manager, the wonderful woman who I thought would be sympathetic to my plight.

"Merry Christmas," I said to her.

"Merry Christmas to you too."

"I love how you decorated the place, with the tree in the recreation room and the lights and decorations."

"Oh thanks. We like to do this for the residents."

"I was wondering if I could talk to you about something. I'm a little low on funds now, with the holidays and all, and I'm not going to have enough money for a full month's rent. I'm going to have to go back to a weekly payment schedule for a while."

"It costs more that way."

"I know, I just don't have a choice. I think I'll get this new job I interviewed for and that'll be more money, but not right away."

She smiled at me and I wasn't sure why. "You're a good person to have here. No trouble and you dress nice. I'll give you the first week of the year free. You think you can come up with the monthly rent by the tenth?"

"Oh yes, I can do that."

"Okay, let's do that."

"Thank you," I said. "Thanks so much. I appreciate it."

"Of course. We want you to stay."

She opened the guest book to make these notes regarding my account and I headed back to my room, content in knowing that I would be able to stay there, with my friends. I figured that I might be able to come up with the money because I was expecting my severance check from the cable company and that added to the money had should add up to what I needed. Things would work out after all and I was glad that I had told her my situation and explained everything to her.

A few days later I got a call from the big media company and they wanted to interview me a second time and I knew this was a good sign. This was the first week of January and that night was my last night of training at the cable company and I was finally ready to begin work for them, but I knew for certain that I was going to get this new advertising job at the big media company so I stopped going to the cable guy and felt a lot better at not having to go to a seedy part of Hollywood every day and work for the giant cable company. I remembered one of the training days in the last week of training when we were assigned to someone in the call center to listen to some calls from real customers to real representatives, and I was assigned to this one lady and sat with her and we needed a supervisor for a call and both of us stood up to look for one and I looked across the vast sea of cubicles that extended forever and all I could see was row after row of customer service people in their tiny little cubicles and I swear that I could not see an end to all the rows. The main floor was so long that I couldn't even see the wall at the other side of the building because it was so very far away. That was when I felt like just another worker in a giant maze of workers and bugs and cells and I didn't even feel human and that was when I knew that I had to quit, that I wouldn't be able to work like that for so long, in such an impersonal environment. I just couldn't do it, no not at all.

I went back to the advertising company two days later and participated in a group interview with two other applicants, who were being interviewed for different positions than me, and two interviewers. I didn't like this type of interview at all but I did and said what I thought the company representatives wanted to hear.

I was now out of work at the beginning of the year, which normally would have been just awful, but I received my last check, severance really, from the cable job and then had enough for rent for January and paid it and felt a hell of a lot better, though I had very little left for gas and food.

I got a call the next day with a job offer from the media company and of course I accepted it and then felt better than ever. I calculated the days I would work after I started and it looked like I would get paid by the beginning of February and have enough for rent for that month and that was great news to me for sure.

On my first day the new employees had their pictures taken for the ID cards and I felt silly with my black hair and couldn't believe how silly I had been in thinking that I had had tuberculosis and that the end of my life was near. Even after the x-ray proved negative, I had still thought the worst, though maybe all this was because I was so down-and-out in December, because I quit the cable job and didn't have another job to replace it. And maybe there were other things going on in my life then, too.

But the new job seemed great and there was a wonderful, friendly blonde girl who worked in the room where I was assigned, and she was as kind as could be and really befriended me and helped me feel welcome and made my transition into the position quite easy and she was a big reason for why I stayed at the company for nearly half a year, a whole half of a year if you can believe it, and to me that's a long time indeed.

2

I grew tired of my black hair real fast and wanted a change to go along with the new year, so I walked south a few blocks and found this cool little barber shop. I walked in and could tell that everyone was Hispanic and I wondered if I needed to know Spanish, but one of the workers waved me over to his chair and so I felt better. But then he started to speak Spanish and I had to shake my head.

"Yo hablo poquito Espanol, pero no mucho," I said to him.

"Oh sorry," he said. "I thought you were Mexican. Maybe because of the dark hair and this neighborhood I'm in."

"It's all right. Actually, my true hair color is blonde so I'd like to get my hair cut really short so you can't see the black any more."

"Did you dye it?"

"Yeah, I was in a dark mood."

"It's okay. I'll get you back to normal."

And soon he did just that and I walked back to the hotel and felt like a different and better person without all that black hair. My hair was very short now but I knew it would grow out soon enough.

I found out a few days later that Harry and Dave had moved rooms, from one on the east side of the building to a room on the west side.

"Why did you do that?" I asked Dave.

"Oh, just for a change. I was tired of it over there."

They had actually moved to the side of the building where my Japanese friends from my first month at the hotel used to live, and I started to wonder what happened to them and how they were doing in New York and what they were doing there and if they were ever going to come back.

Around the middle of January I was eating downstairs in the cafeteria and then started to leave when Shizu approached me.

"Sakura has come back," she said.

"Really?" I asked.

"Yes, you want to see her?"

"Yeah." I knew that I had treated her poorly during the previous two months and I wondered if she would speak to me again, but I figured that I had to try.

"She's in the lobby. Come on."

So I followed Shizu to the lobby and looked around and spotted Sakura near the front desk and went over to speak to her.

"Welcome back," I said. I waited for her response.

She turned around and looked prettier than I had ever seen her before and I could tell that she had either gained or lost some weight and that either way it made her look better.

"Thank you," she said as she smiled.

"Are you in the same room?" I asked.

"Oh yes, they saved it for me."

"Good, good. I'll call you."

"Yes, please do."

And then I left her with her paperwork at the desk and went back to my room. I had mixed feelings about her return but mostly I felt good and was happy to have her back. I was a bit confused over how anxious Shizu was in getting me to see her again, of telling me that Sakura had returned, especially given the times I had flirted with Shizu. But Sakura being back was a great thing indeed and maybe Shizu had learned how I had treated

Sakura and actually wanted us to be friends again. Sometimes I couldn't tell if Shizu was more nice and kind or mean and devious. I couldn't tell for sure and maybe that was one of the things that I found attractive about her.

I went over to her room later that night.

"I'm glad you're back," I said as we sat on the bed and chatted.

"I had to come back twice. I'm so stupid."

"No you're not. What happened?"

"I came back to the U.S. to come to the hotel again and then the airport people checked my papers and my visa had expired. I couldn't believe it. I was so stupid not to have checked it."

"You just forgot. What else?"

"They took me with some other people and made us wait for a few hours and then I had to fly all the way home again."

"Your parents were angry, I suppose."

"Yes, very mad. They almost wouldn't let me come back. The plane ticket is expensive."

"I'm sure it is," I said.

"Oh, that reminds me. You remember Rumi?"

"You're friend, if you call it that. She and Shizu had said those things about you."

"Yes. She needs some help."

"So? Don't you remember what she said?"

"That's okay. She's still my friend. Can you help her confirm her flight?"

"I can if you want me to," I said.

"I do. She's really nervous about the ticket."

"Okay. Just have her call me with the ticket info and I'll call the airline."

"Thank you, I'll tell her."

"I'll go back to my room. Maybe we can do something together in the evening in the next few days."

"Yes, I'd like that."

So I went back to my room and in a few minutes Rumi called and at first I didn't want to help her at all but as she explained her ticket problem and the whole predicament with how she had changed dates and times I began to feel empathy for her and decided to be kind about it. I got all the info I needed and called the airline and was able to conform that everything was in order and that Rumi's ticket was valid. I called Rumi back later and explained that everything was fine and she was extremely grateful for the help.

3

I knew I needed to make things better with Sakura because I actually felt bad about the things I had done and how I had treated her. I still cared for her, maybe now more than ever, and I didn't want to be without her. We started to go out to different places in the city, to the movies, to the beaches, to restaurants, and every other place we could imagine. We went to Chinatown and Little Tokyo and close by the library downtown. We went all over.

But I liked Shizu too and did things with her whenever I could. There were fun nights in Shizu's room with her, Sakura, Harry, and me. One night we drove to a neighborhood Chinese restaurant, the one I often went to, the one with the Hispanic employees who sold Chinese food in Koreatown, and we brought the food back and ate it in Shizu's room and it was a perfectly cool night and the four of us enjoyed each other's company and everything was great in our lives and we were full of hope and nothing bothered us, not a single thing at all, and I was completely content, being in that room with Sakura and Shizu, and I knew that Shizu knew that I liked her more than I liked Sakura, and Shizu knew that she liked Harry more than me, and Shizu was happy, it seemed, with two guys who wanted her affection, and maybe she wanted Sakura out of the picture or maybe not. But I knew that Shizu knew all this so I did what she didn't want me to do, and that was that I always sat close to Sakura and was always kind to her and always made sure that Shizu heard me when I planned something great with Sakura for the next day, maybe a trip to Malibu after a great lunch at a nice restaurant. This is how it was and this is the truth.

And always, after these complicated get-togethers, I would leave with Sakura and we would go back to my room and things would happen and we would have a great time and she would ask if she could stay the night in my room and I always said no and I didn't know why at the time but maybe I know why now, maybe it makes more sense in retrospect.

Things got better with Sakura, and things also got better with Shizu and occasionally I went to her room and met Harry there and we would go out on the town and do things together and talk about other films he wanted to make. And of course I would help him write whatever he was working on.

"I'd ask Jose to help me write these," Harry told me, "but he says he wants to focus on writing a book."

"Really?" I asked.

"Yeah, but he always says the same thing, that he's only finished two paragraphs so far."

"Maybe books take longer. I'll help you any time with the scripts."

Harry continued work on his short films but we never did any more actual filming, just work on scripts and ideas and stuff like that. The last movie we had done was "Shakedown 1999" and that seemed an eternity ago, but it had come out pretty good, especially the scenes with Jose in the big parking lot, though that was nothing new, that of Jose doing a good job in his role, whatever it was.

I wanted Harry to keep making films but it seemed obvious after a while that he was focusing more on making and planning for a longer film. I was excited about "Dirty Laundry" and wanted to get it done right away because I knew that half the work was just getting everyone together. So I would always give Harry more details about where we could shoot it, not planned for the area near the laundry room, and we went over every scene and planned for who would do what role. But Harry just didn't do it and wouldn't set a date and I had no idea why and he kept giving excuses so I started to give up. It was the one student film I liked the most, partly because I had written it but mostly because it seemed to have the most potential. There were fights in it and a love triangle and blood and a get-away and a bunch of other stuff that made it interesting.

During this time of my trying to get Harry to get it done or plan a date, I found out that he had started living in Shizu's room. He kept all his stuff in Dave's room because the hotel management had a policy against non-married young students staying in the same room, but nobody really cared about the rule and it was never enforced.

So he started living in her room and spending most of his time there and that was fine by me because I got to spend time with her too because I was always working with Harry. I still liked Shizu even though I was dating Sakura. And the best times would be when Sakura and I would plan something really grand for the evening and mention it to Harry and Shizu and I could see them get jealous because they didn't have a car like I did and this couldn't get around and enjoy all the places like Sakura and I could. So you know I related all of our trips and dates to Shizu because I knew how jealous she got.

There was this whole troubled relationship I had with Shizu and Harry and half of it could be traced to the fact that he had gotten to her before I could. I liked Sakura but I really liked Shizu and couldn't stand the fact that she spent her time and her nights with Harry, because I didn't think he was so great and he couldn't come up with a decent plot for the life of him, and he always came to me after he realized he didn't have a story for one of his films.

One night Harry called me and mentioned that there was a concert at a local hangout and that his friends were part of the band.

"That sounds cool," I said.

"What are you doing tonight?" he asked.

"Oh, just watching television. There's a nature special on." Now I knew that he wanted me to take him and Shizu to the little concert and I knew he didn't like having to ask me to take him, but I didn't want to go and didn't want to take them and certainly wasn't going to volunteer to do so.

"Do you think you could take us?"

"Oh yeah, no problem. When you wanna go?"

"Maybe fifteen minutes."

"All right," I said. "Come to my room when you're ready."

I hung up and called Sakura. "You want to go to see some free music show?"

"With Harry and Sakura?" she asked.

"Well, yes."

"Do we have to? No, it's okay, I'll go."

"Okay, can you come over to my room in a few minutes?"

"I'll see you then. Bye."

She hung up and I got ready and soon there was a knock on my door. I opened it and went into the hallway and locked my door behind me. Harry and Shizu were ready to go.

"Are you ready?" Harry asked me.

"Just waiting for someone. Here she is."

Sakura showed up just then and the four of us looked at each other and I could tell that Shizu hadn't expected Sakura to come.

"Is she coming?" asked Shizu.

"Yes, of course."

"We should throw her in the trash."

Now this surprised the hell out of you and there was silence in the hallway as her words hung in the air. Sakura was stunned and so was I and I'm sure Harry didn't know what to think. She actually said that, she said those words just like that and I'm sure it was because there was something going on inside her, jealousy or whatever, and it surfaced right then and there. I should have turned around and walked out with Sakura, but I didn't. I wanted to go out with Sakura and I wasn't going to let Shizu spoil the evening.

"Let's go," I said. "We don't wanna be late."

So Harry and I chatted and so did Sakura and Shizu as we walked out to the parking lot. And then as I drove south to wherever the place was located, I could hear Shizu and Sakura talk in the back seat and it was in Japanese and I wondered how Sakura was able to be so polite after what Shizu had said, and then I remembered how Japanese people are usually really polite and considerate yet I was still confused and befuddled by everything. And as Harry told me where to go, all I could do was think back to when Sakura and I had finally let Yasu and Shizu into Sakura's room that one night, back when we had been passionate all evening and had never answered the door or the phone until Yasu had banged on it really hard and as Shizu had yelled and we couldn't avoid them any more, and they came in and it was terribly awkward when they realized what had been happening in the room yet both of them had still been polite and courteous, especially Shizu, though Yasu mostly just covered his face with his long hair in utter disbelief at that whole, crazy situation. That's all I could think of as I drove to the silly, dumb, little concert with Harry beside me and Shizu and Sakura acting all friendly in the back. That's all I could think of, if you can believe it.

4

It surprised all of us when Yasu came back to the hotel to visit us one day.

"I can't believe you flew here from Seattle," said Jose. "I'd never come back if I got away."

It seemed obvious to me that Yasu had come back because he was lonely, that he didn't know anyone yet in Seattle and didn't have anyone to hang out with. But that didn't seem to justify coming all the back to Koreatown. I was surprised most by the fact that he hadn't even called to let me know that he was coming. I just happened to see him watching TV with Jose in the lobby on my way out.

"How long are you here?" I asked.

Yasu didn't respond to me and I just looked at him and then looked over at Jose.

"Yasu, Darrin's talking to you," said Jose to him. I'm sure Jose was confused over why Yasu had ignored me, but then Jose didn't like Yasu too much and he knew that I was dating Sakura. I'm sure Jose had things figured out. Besides, there was the time in January when everyone was gone except me, Jose and Sakura, and I had come down for breakfast and Sakura had been sitting alone at a table and Jose alone at another table and I had had to make a decision as to where to sit and of course I chose my girlfriend. So Jose was aware of some things, though not all.

"Just for the weekend," said Yasu.

"How is it up there?"

"Oh good. My host family is very nice, but I don't like living in the same town as my sister."

Now this confused me because she had been living there before him so I couldn't see why he moved up there at all.

"Hey, could you do me a favor?" I asked him. I knew that he probably wouldn't because of our strained relationship, because of how he disliked my going out with Sakura and dating her.

"Yes, what?"

"I've heard there are some offices in Seattle for canneries that operate in Alaska where I want to go work soon. See if you can find some and maybe I can apply by mail."

"I'll look for them."

I had a feeling he wouldn't find anything because I barely knew what to look for and I doubted that he would have much of a clue, given that he didn't know what I was talking about. But I asked him nonetheless.

Somehow the conversation turned to Sakura.

"I heard she flew here from Japan and then had to go right back home because her visa had expired."

"That's right," I said.

"That's so dumb of her. It's stupid. How could she not know?"

Now, it wasn't so much that Yasu said this, because I expected him to do so, but it was how he said it that bothered me the most and made me hate him. He said it with pleasure and happiness and took great pride in the words. And he said it while looking away from me, without making eye contact, which made it a totally cowardly act on his part. So he said what he wanted to say and that was the end of everything and I never saw him again and never spoke to him again and I'm sure that was what he wanted so I was happy to oblige. And as I walked away from him on this day, I thought back to when we first met, when he had wanted me to help teach him English and be his tutor and that really made me laugh, because of all the different things that had happened between us that had nothing to do with learning the language, nothing at all.

5

I spent lots of time with Dave and Jose, that is whenever I wasn't with Sakura. Half the time I was in denial with them that I was dating Sakura, not so much because of her but because of how much disdain hey had for Harry and his constant talk of Shizu and how great she was, and I didn't want to be like that in any way.

Dave, Jose and I spent a lot of time at the local fast food restaurants because the food there was inevitably better than that which was served in the hotel cafeteria, which we had to pay for whether we wanted it or not. We would also go to the bowling alley nearby and just play video games and just spend the spare money we had and just hang out and have fun. We would go to Santa Monica and walk up and down Third Street and go to the beach and one time we stopped at the McDonald's there on the way back and Jose whispered to me that I was standing next to some celebrity and I didn't believe him until people went up to her and asked her for her autograph. But I made sure not to look at her directly because I didn't want her to feel uncomfortable.

One night Dave and I rode up and down Sunset Boulevard and then all over town and finally got bored and headed back to the hotel where we went to the fire escape and just hung out up there and felt the ocean breeze and marvel at the city lights and how they shined off the palm trees that lined all the neighboring streets, and it was just perfect up there, perfect indeed.

And one evening we had some special guests arrive at the hotel and they were two really pretty girls all the way from Argentina, in their twenties maybe, and the whole gang, me, Dave, and Jose, was downstairs in the recreation room when they arrived and so of course we introduced ourselves and Dave and Jose were completely infatuated and interested and spoke Spanish to them and talked on and on into the night, and I finally got bored and went to my room but not without taking another look at them because they were so fine and tanned and perfectly shaped and had such wonderful, rich accents, and were dressed in grand, normal clothes. Oh, the girls from Argentina made all of our hearts and minds spend that night and the week in which they stayed at the hotel went by faster than you could imagine and Dave skipped a bunch of his classes at the community college to hang out with them and I didn't blame him at all, not one bit.

6

Now Rebecca had spent a whole month or so back home in Sweden and must have gotten back and stayed in her room for a while because I didn't see her at all for a heck of a long time. Finally, down in the cafe, I saw her and approached her and welcomed her back.

"Great to see you," I said. "How long have you been back here?"

"Oh, two weeks."

"What? Where? I haven't seen you."

I saw you a couple times in the morning, when you were all dressed up for work. You get a new job?"

"Yeah, it's nice. I may stay a while."

"Good."

"Let's go do something. How about a drive on Mulholland tonight?"

"Okay, call me when you want to go. I'll bring my camera."

A few hours later I knocked on her door and she grabbed her fancy, expensive camera and we left in my car.

"You should stick with photography," I said. "I love the pictures you've shown me."

"Maybe I will. I don't know."

"Making movies is okay, but photography is quicker and you can do more and get jobs in the field." I believed this.

"Yeah, if you're good."

"You can be good."

So we drove and talked and went up and down Mulholland and stopped occasionally and looked down at the valley and then looked at downtown L.A. and Rebecca took some photos but not too many.

"How's Sylvia?" I asked.

"Okay, but she fights with her boyfriend a lot."

"Does she still live in the hotel?" I ask.

"Yeah. She moved out briefly but then came back."

"Than that was her I heard that night."

"Was she screaming?"

"Yeah," I said. "I thought I recognized her voice. She screamed all night long at some guy and only yelled back once or twice. I nearly called the police because I thought she was getting raped."

"Oh no, they do that a lot. Sometimes when I'm in the room. I don't know why they stay together."

"Me neither. They should know it's not normal for people to scream at each other."

"What do you mean?" asked Rebecca.

"What? Most people don't scream as a means of normal conversation."

"Yeah they do."

And then it got really weird because Rebecca started trying to convince me that people do scream and yell at each other and that it's normal and good.

"You shouldn't keep all those things inside," she explained. "You should let them out."

I figured that her family lived like that so I knew right then that I couldn't very well convince her that it was wrong or abnormal or dysfunctional, so I just let it be and we had fun for the rest of the evening and decided to do more things with each other as we could.

"You hear about Harry?" I asked her.

"That he moved into an apartment with his Danish friend? Yeah, good for him."

"Sounds like the place is pretty far from here."

"Yeah, but he does what he does."

"True. Hey, thanks for the evening. Let's do this again, and tell me how the pictures turn out."

"Thanks a lot," she said as we separated in the hotel hallway.

"Any time at all," I replied. "Any time, my good, easy Swedish friend."

"Not all Swedish girls are easy," she said jokingly. We had shared a joke about how Swedish girls were stereotyped as being easy when it came to sex.

"I'm patient," I yelled back. Of course we were just friends. I had learned my lesson with Rebecca when I made a pass at her once in my room and she jumped back, yelled "We're just friends!", and raced out of my room and back to hers. I resolved back then not to try that again with her because of how well we got along and how I didn't want to lose her friendship.

7

The days were warm and long and I continued to work at the media company on Sunset Boulevard, though I never had much to do. My supervisor was brand new in her position and I was pretty new in mine and she didn't want me to screw anything up, because it would reflect poorly on her, so she didn't give me any work and I was responsible for nothing. So I pretended to look busy and typed meaningless words and letters into the computer and waited in the fax room for imaginary faxes that never came and copied papers and files that were supposed to be thrown away. I had to look busy with no work and that's what I did. I worked at a huge advertising company and got paid well and did nothing and produced nothing and learned nothing and nobody seemed to care and I wondered what the hell was wrong with the situation.

So my escape was my life at the apartment and I did things with Sakura and talked of movies with Harry and hung out with Dave and Jose.

I called Dave one night and he was in his room so I went over to visit.

"Come," he said after I knocked on the door.

"What's going on?" I asked as I entered and walked around.

"Not much. Harry went to see some dumb movie."

"Yeah, he does that a lot." I sat down on Harry's bed and there was stuff all over and on top of it. "Does he use this bed at all?" I asked.

"He sleeps with Shizu, you know that?"

"Well, I thought sometimes."

"He doesn't sleep here any more. Just puts his stuff down and clutters up the place with his stupid movie equipment."

I got up and looked out the windows. "One thing I like about this building is the view. Especially out on the fire escapes. And on the roof. You never see these neon lights in other cities."

"Mental," grumbled Dave. "It's a mental hospital. Greasy food too."

Both of us laughed at this because it had become the running joke, that of Dave always complaining about the place and calling it a mental hospital. "Cockroaches and crazy people, and crappy food."

"You seem a little grumpier than normal," I said. "Something the matter?"

"I don't know, no. I just miss the Argentina girls, and I can't get 'em outta my head. Both of them. Why did they leave?"

"You could write to them."

"Naw, too long. Maybe they wouldn't even get it. I've just gotta get over them."

"They were awfully nice."

"They were better than nice. I should've made a move or tried to talk to them more. Now they're gone. Damn. Mental hospital. Crazy here."

I thought about all this and it reminded me of something in my life, a great love that I had never gotten over, an obsession that was on my mind constantly, an obsession with a fabulous girl named Claire, a person whom I admired and respected and longed for terribly.

"All right, you going to dinner tonight?" I asked Dave.

"I can't eat. I don't want to eat."

I laughed. "I'll stop by later for Married with Children."

I made it to the door and glanced back and it was quite obvious that Dave was quite enamored with those cute girls from Argentina. As I walked back to my room, I replayed in my mind those great nights when they were at the hotel, when the whole gang hung out with them in the recreation room, when I was stunned by how beautiful and exotic and tanned they were. I missed them a lot too. But I'm sure Dave missed them more than me. When you miss someone so much that it makes you green and sick, then you know you miss them a lot.

I entered my room and sat down. Dave's talk had gotten to me and I couldn't resist any longer. It had been a very long time since I had heard my obsession's voice and I just had to call her. I knew there was a chance she would be there, in her apartment, and thus might answer the phone and I would have to have something to say to her, but it was a Friday and I knew she was probably out on the town wherever she lived so I dialed her east coast number. The last time I had dialed it was back in Beverly Hills when I was with Keith that one night.

The phone rang and I became more nervous and felt it in my stomach. Finally, luckily, an answering machine picked up and I could hear her voice and it was as beautiful as it had always been and I nearly cried and the beep sounded and there was nothing I could say so I didn't say anything and just hung up. There was nothing I could do. I lived my life and she lived hers, far, far away, and it was torture to think that she lived so very far away and I didn't know if I would ever see her again. And I knew exactly how Dave felt because I felt it too. I felt it so much that I wasn't hungry either because food couldn't make us feel better. Dave missed his Argentinean girls and I missed Claire and both of us were made miserable by our passions. And we couldn't eat and didn't want to sleep and only wanted our obsessions back in our lives, and we wondered how we would make it in life with these people in our hearts and in our heads. It seemed impossible.

8

I went downstairs to the recreation room and played the Blood Brothers video game when I heard someone walk down the steps behind me. I turned around and recognized my good friend.

"Lugo! Where have you been?" I walked over and shook his hand. "I haven't seen you in forever."

"I've been working, in the movies. I got this one part I'm very excited about. The director had the camera right in front of me and everything."

"Wow, what's it called?"

"I don't know. Something with an X in the title. It's a lot different than regular movies. Have you seen David or Jose?"

"No, they're both not here. I just checked their rooms."

"Me too. I called them."

"What are you doing here?" I asked. "It's great to see you."

"The volcano movie is out now."

"I know, I want to see it."

"It's that movie from last year I was in."

"What?" I wasn't sure what he was talking about.

"Remember, when I went down to MacArthur Park at night, when I asked you to come."

I thought about it. "Oh yeah. That was Volcano?"

"Yeah."

"Oh, man. I wish I would have done it now. You wanna go watch the movie?"

"Yes."

"Then let's go. I'm ready. Let me go up and get the paper for the movie times. I'll be right back." I bounced up the steps and was back within two minutes. Lugo was waiting by the front desk. "We're in luck. There's a show starting in an hour. Wanna go the Universal Citywalk to see it?"

"Sure."

As I drove to the theater, Lugo and I talked about what each of us had been doing.

"Do you think we'll be able to see you in the movie?" I asked.

"I don't know. I hope so."

"I should've been in it with you. I regret it now."

"It's so funny," said Lugo. "You know that star in the movie?"

"Tommy Lee Jones?"

"Yeah, see he was walking on the set that night and I lifted up that yellow police tape so he could get through. He liked that and let me be in the scene with the women, and me and my friend got to be up close."

Then we watched the movie and Lugo could be seen all over the place near the park, at least five different times. The movie was great bit even greater because Lugo was in it and the film had been shot close to the apartment building. We headed back to my car after it was done.

"That's so cool," I said. "Your face was huge up on the screen like that. It was so funny."

"And that part where I tied the police line tape on my black friend's forehead, we had done that on the street for fun and the director had us do it for real."

"And then I saw you like three times after that, running all over with that stolen stuff."

"Yeah, we did that all night. It was easy. You should be an extra because it's good money and fun work."

"I know, I should have."

"You still can."

"I'll think about it. I can't wait until it comes out on video so we can pause it when you come on the screen."

We went back to the apartment and by then Dave and Jose had come back and so me and Lugo talked about the movie and how Lugo was in it and how he was a thief during the riots in the streets near the parks. We talked on and on about how cool it was and it was a great day in L.A., a great time in Koreatown with my friends.

9

It was May and Harry and Shizu got some free tickets to Hawaii and decided to go.

"Would you take us to the airport?" he asked me the day before.

"Sure, no problem."

So the next day I helped them with their stuff and drove them to the airport and dropped them off.

"Have a great time," I said as I left them with their luggage.

"We're a bit early," Harry said to Shizu.

"It's better to be early," I said.

I knew he was thinking of asking me something but I didn't want to stick around any more, especially not with Shizu. It was uncomfortable because she knew that I liked her and of course so did Harry and it was all a bit too much to handle so I took off as soon as I could.

"Have a great time and send me a postcard!" I said as I drove off.

I glanced at them in my rearview mirror and they waved good-bye to me as they started to move their luggage. It was strange for me being up on the second level of the airport because my job at LAX had been at the bottom level, the arrivals section, and not up with the departure terminals.

I got back to my room in the hotel building and laid down on my bed to take a nap. My sleep was interrupted by a phone call so I answered it.

"It's Harry," said the caller.

"Hey, you on the plane yet?" I asked.

"No. The flight's been delayed a couple hours."

"Oh. Well, I hope you have fun when you get there."

Then there was silence on the other end for a moment. I already knew what Harry was going to say before he said it.

"Shizu wants to know if you can come pick us up and take us to the beach for an hour."

It was so pathetic of him to pin the request on Shizu, even if it was her idea. There was no way in hell that I was going to drive all the damn way to the damn airport to pick them up and drive them to the damn beach for a damn hour.

"That's a long drive," I said. "By the time I picked you up and we got to the beach, we'd have to leave and go back to the airport. I'm sorry, but I can't."

"Oh, that's okay. We just wanted to ask. It's a long wait for the flight to leave."

I couldn't have cared less how long they had to wait in the terminal. They were on their way to Hawaii, for pete's sake, so they could wait a few hours before the plane took off for paradise.

"Well, have a great time and remember your suntan lotion."

"We will. Bye, Darrin."

I hung up and couldn't believe the two of them. Maybe it had been Shizu's idea to have me go to the airport to do something for them. Maybe she wanted my company and maybe she just wanted to use me and figured that I liked her so much that I wouldn't mind driving all over the damn metropolitan area just to make her happy. I didn't like her that much.

I couldn't sleep any more so I called Sakura and asked her if she wanted to go see for a movie. She said yes and soon we were on our way.

The next day I went over and hung out with Dave for a while.

"I took Harry and Shizu to the airport yesterday for their trip," I said. "And then they wanted me to drive back and take'em to the beach when their plane got delayed."

"They can take a taxi."

"Right, exactly right."

"Hey, we can get into their room if you want."

"Okay." This appealed to me because I wanted to see if I could find anything of Shizu's that might explain how she felt about me or Sakura or Harry for that matter.

"Let's go," said Dave.

The building was exceptionally quiet on this weekend and there was hardly anybody around. We went over to their room.

"You have a key?" I asked.

"No, don't need one. I use a credit card."

"That doesn't work, not on these rooms."

"No, it does. Jose and I did it when he locked himself out."

"Okay, let's try it," I said.

Dave pulled out his card and I watched the hallways and signaled him whenever someone showed up, which only happened one time. He seemed to have some trouble with the lock and couldn't get it to open for twenty minutes.

"Let's go," I said, having gotten tired of waiting.

"Almost got it. Right now."

He twisted the card and pulled up on the doorknob and finally it opened and the two of us went inside the room quickly and shut it behind us. But then once inside we really had no idea what to do and basically lost interest in being there.

I looked around and found something of Shizu's that I was interested in which was a small transparent purse that contained all of her letters from her friends. I flipped through them as I looked for something, anything that was significant in some way.

"Let's go," said Dave. "It's boring here."

I couldn't believe how Dave had been so willing to break in and after two minutes he wanted to get out of there.

"What's wrong?" I asked.

"Nothing."

I scanned through Shizu's letters and finally found one and it was the letter I wrote to her right after she got involved with Harry. I had nearly forgotten about it altogether. It was the letter with the short story about how I had lost Shizu, though I had put the words in the context of Shizu being lost in the big city. The words and lines were still potent for me and I could still feel the loss of her and after I read it again I no longer wanted to be near her stuff and in her room.

"Let's go," I said after I put the letters back.

We walked out and made sure the door was locked again. Then we went down for dinner and never mentioned what we had done to anyone else.

10

I got lucky one day at the company and won a ticket for a great seat to watch the Lakers play game three of a playoff series at the Great Western Forum.

Some of the other guys at work tried to get me to sell them my ticket, but I know that it was valuable if only for the experience.

The ticket was somewhere like the tenth row and close to the opposition team's bench. I got there and it was a great seat and the spot next to mine had been given to a very cute girl who worked in the advertising department, like me, of our company, though I never saw her much during the work day except for in the fax room where I hung out a lot.

"I'm a real big Lakers fan," she said once she arrived and joined me. "So I hope you like to get excited for the game."

"I do," I said, and that was true. The seats were awesome and the place was heavy in intensity because it was game three of the playoffs against the Jazz and they had won the first two games of the series and so the Lakers and the Forum was hungry for a win.

"I've always followed the Lakers and I know a lot about them," she said. "I was a fan when back when Michael Johnson played."

"You mean Magic?" I asked, finding humor in her self-contradiction.

"Yes, Magic. I loved it when he played with those other guys."

"Kareem and Worthy?"

"Yeah," those guys.

Obviously this girl liked to talk about being a fan, but she surely didn't know that much about the team or at least couldn't remember at that point in time. The game proceeded and the Lakers got a good lead but then Shaq got ejected for some reason. It didn't matter because the Lakers were winning and continued to lead by a sufficient margin. The best part of the night was when I saw James Worthy in the stands nearby and it was great to be so close to him.

The night went on and we had a great time and I enjoyed the seats but figured that I would never pay to go to a basketball game in the future because it got too boring and I was much more accustomed to watching it on television. This free ticket made me feel better about the company and I decided to work hard the following week and that's what I did, even though I didn't have much to do.

Soon after this game I couldn't handle working at the advertising media company any more. It seemed pointless because I never did anything and got paid for nothing and maybe that sounds great to other people, the complete lack of work, but it doesn't sound great to me. I hated it because I like to keep busy.

I missed the blonde girl I had worked with in the office. Though I hadn't seen her much because of the big divider between us, I had talked to her a lot and she had seemed like an awfully nice person and really made my days easier, though a lot of the time she didn't talk at all and I wondered how she kept busy. Maybe it had been good that there had been a divider there so she couldn't see how very little work I had done, though that hadn't been my fault at all. But this girl had left the company for a better job somewhere else and I hadn't blamed her for doing so and had actually been jealous of her for being able to do so,

My boss left for her ten-day vacation and, thankfully, she left me with a bunch of work to do, though I didn't see why she hadn't give me some of it before she left. Then a replacement employee came for the girl who had left and it was this nice guy who used to be a stockbroker in another high-rise building in L.A. and who was originally from the east coast. It didn't surprise me that this guy was really into Hollywood and that he was working on screenplays and trying to make it big. We became pals quickly. I asked him all kinds of questions about what it's like being a stockbroker and why he left that occupation. And I found out he was from Philadelphia and that he had gone to the historic boxing center called the Blue Horizon. I had heard quite a lot about the place but had never met someone who had actually been there.

"There's all kinds of celebrities along Sunset Boulevard," he said one day. I knew that he was just like a lot of other people in town who were aspiring to be a part of the entertainment business and trying to make it rich through the sale of their screenplay. It bored me to tears because I had seen it too many times, from those people who called us at Premiere to hype their movie and say how great it was, to Keith and his job at a TV show, to the Russian cab drivers at the airport with their screenplays, to Lugo and Harry and everybody else under the sun, and finally me. I was sick of L.A. and Hollywood and I didn't want to be there any more. I wanted to be around real people with real jobs.

Game six of this same playoff series was on the big screen TV in the recreation room in the building one night in late May and I had a feeling that the Jazz would win, and so I made a bet with the young desk clerk guy. My friends and I watched it in the recreation room and he watched it on the TV near the counter as he had to work.

"I prefer watching it here instead of at the Forum," I said. "It's more comfortable and doesn't cost anything."

"Did you have good seats at the game?" asked Jose.

"Yeah, like five rows behind the Jazz bench. It was great and the girl I was with was real cute. I guess I've gotten used to watching it on TV too much."

"Those seats must have been expensive."

"No doubt. I never would have paid for them."

And then the night wore on and somehow the Jazz beat the Lakers on a last second three-point shot by John Stockton and then I got excited and raced to the front and gladly took my five bucks from the desk clerk. It was a good night of basketball and hanging out with my friends and I liked my life and had no desire to leave, though things would change in the next two weeks.

11

My Japanese friends came back to the hotel in April and they had changed completely, and for the absolute worst and what happened to them tore me apart. I had seen some of them in the hallway and had asked the desk clerk for their room number and he gave it to me and I called.

"Hello," said Bruce.

"Hey, this is Darrin. I heard that you guys came back from New York."

"Oh yes, but maybe just for a short while."

He sounded different. "Can I come over and talk to you?"

"Sure, but I may have to leave quickly."

"I'll be right there." I hung up and ran down the hallway and found the number which was on the east side of the building, in a new room. I knocked and he opened the door and I nearly didn't recognize the person in front of me. He invited me in and I went and sat down on one of the apartment's chairs. I tried not to stare at him and just talk but it was difficult because he looked totally different. Gone were his soft, youthful, plump cheeks and pleasant appearance. Instead, there were pock marks all over his sunken and shallow cheeks and I knew immediately that he and his friends had gotten involved with drugs and that he had been using them for a while.

"How was New York?" I asked.

"Fine, good."

"Did you do lots of stuff?"

He answered but not with any sort of certain response. He was distracted and nervous and agitated. I couldn't believe it was the same person because of how totally different and ugly he looked, terrible beyond belief. Five months earlier he had been the exact image of a young Bruce Lee and I had told him this a number of times and had been excited about making a short film with him and we had written it together and had planned on doing it. And then a month after that, when everyone had come back from a road trip, we had gone to the wedding in Long Beach with Lugo and everyone else and it had been a splendid affair. And now, unbelievably, all of that innocence and vigor had been totally depleted from him and I couldn't stand to look at him any more.

His phone rang just then. He picked it up, said one word in Japanese, listened, and then put down the phone quickly and stood up fast. "I have to go, right now."

I got up as he did and made my way to the door and he was out before I was and down the hallway by the time I pulled his door shut. I figured that he was an addict now and his other friends had called him to either buy some more drugs or to do them in their room. Either way, it was horrible and made me nauseous and I couldn't believe it, I just couldn't. I should have kept everyone in L.A. and co-signed that apartment lease for them and maybe they wouldn't have moved to New York and wouldn't have gotten involved in such a wretched and wasteful life. I had done some smoking with them and certainly some drinking but I never thought they would progress so quickly to other, more addictive drugs. It was downright scary.

A few nights later I was out in the lobby. The desk clerk, a man in his early thirties with a thick mustache, was out near the entrance with Jose and I joined them.

"Did you hear the police sirens?" he asked me.

"No, why?"

"Another shooting, I think. There was one last week near the Taco Bell on the corner and these two people were killed in the parking lot."

"That's a little too close to home," I said. "I won't be going there any more."

"Taco Hell is more like it," said Jose.

It was a rough neighborhood. "I still can't get used to the police helicopters," I said. "Whenever they come around it's like they're looking for someone who lives here in the hotel. They shine their lights right into my room. I'd call the police but they are the police so I don't think anything would be done."

"It's this neighborhood," said the clerk. "It's too awful and there's too many drugs."

"I'm going to move soon," said Jose.

"Me too," I added.

"You better do it soon. Some guys just moved back in and I know they got involved in something."

"You mean the Japanese guys, the ones who moved to New York?" I asked.

"Yeah, you remember them?"

"Sure I do. I was great friends with them last fall, when I first moved here. They were the first people I knew. I even went to the wedding."

"That's them. Did you see that one guy?" he asked.

"Bruce?"

"I don't know his name but he looks bad."

"I call him Bruce because he used to look just like Bruce Lee."

"That's the one."

"Yeah, it's horrible. I was up in his room a few days ago and I could barely tell it was him because his face was so destroyed. I only recognized him from his voice."

"I couldn't believe it when they checked back in. They've gotta be into some real dangerous drugs."

"I know, I know. Maybe if I had co-signed for them on that rental thing."

"Oh no. They asked me to do that too, but you can't take that risk. I wouldn't do that for some of my relatives, let alone some strangers."

"Who are these people?" asked Jose.

"Some Japanese guys who live on the second floor on the west side, underneath Shizu and David's floor."

"I don't know them."

As we talked out front, I thought back to when I first met them and how young and vibrant they had seemed and now their lives had been changed for the worse.

"They must have come from wealthy families, I said, "because they certainly never worked during their time here. I guess they had too much money."

"I don't work but I stay away from that kind of stuff," said Jose.

"I think I'd like not having to worry about money. I nearly had to move out in January because I didn't have any money and barely had money to live on."

"Why didn't you tell me?" asked Jose. "I could've given you some cash. My parents could have sent me a lot more."

And then I remembered that Jose hadn't worked and hadn't gone to a school and had surely had his parents support him during his time in L.A., so much so that he had all the time in the world to write a book though he never got very far.

"I didn't even think to ask you."

"You better tell me the next time you need money. I can help."

"Thanks, I appreciate it. Maybe if those guys had had it like me, they wouldn't have had the funds to turn to heroin or whatever it was they started using."

"Maybe," said the desk clerk. "I just can't believe the change."

It was dark outside but a cool breeze had come in and cooled us off as we stood out near the entrance and contemplated the hotel and the city and our place in everything. I marveled at that had happened with my friends and all that had changed in such a short time, and I remembered how I might have been able to prevent some of it if I had co-signed on the rental application with my Japanese friend. But I knew I couldn't do that because I would have been held responsible if they took off and that wasn't a chance I wanted to take.

12

In late April, after dinner, I saw Rumi come down the main steps in the lobby with her luggage. Harry and Shizu were with her. Sakura was with me and all of a sudden the whole gang was right there in the lobby, except for Dave and Jose who weren't really a part of this group.

"Are you leaving?" I asked her.

"Yes, time to go. Can I get a picture of you, the group of you?"

I really didn't feel like it, but Rumi had been at the hotel for a while and had been a part of our circle and I wanted things to end on a good note.

"Sure," I said. Sakura stood by me as Harry and Shizu stood together next to us and Rumi took a few pictures and I wondered how significant that picture was and how I wanted a copy of it for posterity. Harry and I grabbed her bags and took them out to the waiting taxi and then she was off to the airport and I didn't hear from her again and only heard a little bit about her from Sakura a year or two later.

I spent some of the evening in Sakura's room and then went back to mine to think about things. I knew that I was going to be leaving soon and I figured that I could go to Alaska for the summer and work there at a cannery. The advertisement in December for work there had really got me excited about the prospect of an adventure in that section of the country, and every Sunday since then I had scanned the ads but hadn't seen anything having to do with Alaska or work at a cannery. I regretted not having gone to the interview when I had the chance because at the very least I could have gotten some information about the company and maybe I could have used that info later on.

But, instead, I remembered that Harry had casually mentioned something about his friend doing that kind of work and how they had talked about it one time at Harry's community college. I wanted to get in touch with his friend so I called Harry one day.

"Hey, you ever gonna finish those movies?" I asked him.

"I'm working on getting the use of a sixteen millimeter camera. It just takes some time, but I still want to do "Dirty Laundry.""

"Me too," I said. "It'll be great."

"But I want to do it right, and with lighting and good camera work."

To me this meant that he probably wasn't going to do it all because I figured I'd be long gone and so would the others by the time he got everything set up.

"Hey, remember that guy you talked about, the one who had worked in Alaska?"

"Yes, he's in one of my classes."

"I'm interested in doing that now," I said. "If you see him, can you have him call me?"

"Sure. I think I have his number here."

"Great. Can I have it?"

"Okay, let me find it."

I waited and he found it and gave it to me over the phone.

"Can you tell him I'm going to call him so he doesn't think I'm a stranger?"

"Sure, I'll see him tomorrow."

"Okay, great. Let me know when you need me for the film."

"I will."

I hung up and then a few days later I called the number of Harry's friend but he wasn't there then so I had to try back a few more times.

Finally, he was home. I explained who I was and how I wanted to go to Alaska to work.

"Where should I go?" I asked him.

"Go to Kenai. That's where most of the canneries are."

"Is it hard to get work?" I asked.

"No, as long as you go early, before July. June is best. I've worked there for four summers and there's always plenty of work."

"Where do you live?"

"I've always lived in my tent on the company site. But there are places that offer room and board and I'd try and get on with them if you can. Some are very nice."

"Thanks, thanks a lot. Maybe we'll see each other up there."

"Maybe. Glad to help."

I hung up and felt a lot better knowing that it shouldn't be too hard to get work up there. Now I knew for sure that I was going to leave and go there for the summer. I just didn't know when it was going to happen. I thought about calling Yasu to see if he had found out anything about the canneries, but I knew that he hadn't so I didn't waste the money on the call.

Rebecca called me later in the day and asked me if I wanted to do something with her, and of course I did. My mind was on too many things and I couldn't think of anything fun for us to do. I drove her to do some errands and then dropped her off at a friend's place.

"Are you mad at me?" she asked.

"No, no, not at all," I said. "I'm just distracted. My work is awful and I can't get my car registered."

"Oh, I thought I had done something."

"No, no." Right then I had a feeling that this was going to be my last time with her, that I wouldn't see her again after that moment, so I said some things that needed to be said. "Looks like I might move out soon. Rebecca, I want you to know that I like you a lot and hope that we're friends forever. Seriously, I will try hard to stay in touch with you, no matter where each of us goes."

"I feel the same way, more so," she said as she reached over and hugged me.

"But maybe we'll see each other again before I leave."

"I hope so."

She got out and walked away and that was the last time I saw her, until years later when I promised over and over that I would meet her in London and I was finally able to do so. And when I went I took her the very first copy of this book and gave it to her after we hugged for a very long time.

I paid my rent and barely had money left over for food and knew that I wouldn't be able to pay my other bills until I received my next check. Then I realized that I didn't want to pay another month's rent because it was so expensive and I decided that May would be my last month in the hotel. The other thing that made me certain of this was the fact that I couldn't register my car because I couldn't get it smogged. It required lots of repair work to get it smoggable and I didn't have the money to do that. The registration wasn't due until June so I figured it would be best if I went home by the end of May and left my car with my family as I spent the summer in Alaska. Things were starting to come together.

13

I knew what I was doing. I had done it many times before and I could always tell when the circumstances had coalesced to the point where it was time to move on. The rent was going to be due soon and I didn't have the money for it and knew I wasn't going to borrow any more money from my parents. I was tired of L.A. and tired of my job and definitely tired of the hotel and my room there. I had grown weary of the same old routine.

It was a Friday at work and I decided that it was my last day. I went out to lunch with my new friend, my co-worker who worked in the same room as me, and I conveyed my decision to him as we walked back from lunch.

"I don't feel well," I lied.

"Don't quit. This place is great and a lot better than my other job."

"I've been here too long," I said. "It's time to go." I knew he liked it at the company but he was new and didn't have my situation and he was really interested about the movie industry and I had lost most of my interest in it. The only interest I had left in it was the song I liked by Bob Seger about Hollywood nights.

"It'll get better. Just ask your buyer for more work or talk to one of the trainers. They'll help you."

"It's too late for that. There are other things going on in my life besides work. Just do me a favor and tell my buyer that it didn't have anything to do with her because I don't want her to think that even though it's true. She's an awfully nice person."

"Okay," he said. "I'll tell her. But I'd prefer it if you came back on Monday."

He went to his desk and I went to mine. I gathered all the work I had done, everything she had given me to do, and took it over and placed it on her desk along with a note detailing what I had accomplished. Then I gathered my personal things from my desk and slipped out when my co-worker was in the fax room. I didn't see anyone on the way and soon I was in my car and headed south and then east on Wilshire Boulevard.

I go to the hotel building, parked out front, and went up to my room. My stuff had already been packed because I had had a feeling that I would be leaving soon. I took all my stuff to my car and then went and checked out of the hotel and said good-bye to the clerk after I gave him a forwarding address for my mail. I didn't feel like saying good-bye to anyone else because it would have been too weird.

I felt that I knew what I was doing. I had lots of information about Alaska now and how to get jobs there and where to go. And I knew my parents would help me out and let me store my car and belongings at their place for a while. I knew I was going back to Stockton for a few days and that I would get a one-way ticket to Alaska and be headed there by the beginning of the following week, by about the time that someone noticed me missing at work. I would be long gone.

The only thing that bothered me about leaving was Sakura because I figured it might hurt her a bit, the fact that I didn't say good-bye to her or let her know that I was leaving. But I couldn't stand to see her cry again, not after what happened that one night when she cried on my shoulder in her room, so I just started driving up the freeway and tried to get as far away from my life as possible, and that's exactly what I did.

PART 4

Alaska, Arizona and Japan

I

I was home again, but not for very long. Maybe I should have stayed in L.A. and dealt with everything. Maybe I should have told my boss about how I felt about the minuscule amount of work for which I was responsible, about how there was usually nothing for me to do at all, how I was wasting my time being there and accomplishing very little. Then maybe I could have gotten some more work, and felt happier about myself and my place in the company. I could have earned some more money and then I could have gotten my car fixed. At least I should have talked to Sakura before I left and explained why I was leaving. But none of that had happened. I just ran away because it was the easiest thing to do. I just took off and left all my problems behind me and I ran away so I wouldn't have to deal with any of it any more, and in the end I didn't have to because it didn't take me long to get far away and my problems were quickly forgotten and were replaced by new worries and concerns.

"I've decided to go up to Alaska for the summer to work at a fish cannery," I said to my parents when I got home that evening. "That's why I left L.A."

I didn't tell them what other reasons there were, that I was just running from my problems down there, that I had become tired of everything and everybody and couldn't take it any more, couldn't stomach another hour of any of it, and that was why I had left. It was less that I wanted to go to Alaska and more that I wanted to leave Los Angeles.

"Do you know anybody up there?" asked my mom.

"Not really. But I just met some guy down south and he told me where to go and how there's all kinds of work there in Kenai. I have his phone number."

"I've heard about those tent cities they have at the canneries," said my mother. "You can stay in one of those."

"Right, that's my plan. But there are places that offer room and board so I'm going to try and get one of those first if I can. I have this book that tells about all the companies and what they offer and when they hire."

"Are you taking your car?" asked my dad.

"No, I'd like to leave it here until I come back. It needs to be smogged and repaired."

"Sure, that's no problem," said my father. "I'll check it out for you."

"And I doubt if it would make it even as far as Seattle."

"What things are you going to take?" asked my mother.

"Not much. But I need a big backpack or something."

"I've got an old army duffel bag," offered my dad.

"Will it hold a lot?"

"Sure, you can pack a ton into it, just cram it in there. That's what they're designed for."

"Okay, let's use that."

"Do that after we eat," added my mom. "You're not leaving tonight."

Later that night my father found the army bag and we located an old tent, a tarp, some blankets, extra clothes, and other necessities.

"One idea might be to take one of those little carry-all devices with wheels and when you get tired you can just put the duffel bag on it behind you so you won't have to carry it all the time. Just pull it behind you."

"Good idea," I said. "I'll do that."

"Make sure you take lots of warm clothes," said my mother. "You don't know how cold it can get up there. It is Alaska."

"Right."

And so we packed for my big adventure and prepared throughout the weekend. And then I went to a local travel agency and purchased a one-way ticket from Sacramento to Seattle.

"What about your mail?" asked my mom.

"I've had it forwarded here from L.A. Can you keep it until I get an address up in Alaska?"

"Of course."

As I prepared for my journey, I thought about Sakura and how terrible I had been to her, how I had just left her like that without saying goodbye. But part of me knew that our relationship wasn't over yet, that we would still continue our friendship in some fashion, that at some time in the future I would hold her tight against me for the last time. I just knew all this would come to pass. Things were not over between us, even though I was heading off to Alaska and she was staying in L.A., even though eventually she would have to move back home to Japan, even though neither of us knew what was going on in our lives or what our futures held for us. All I knew was that I was getting far away from my most recent past. And all she knew was that I was leaving her.

On Sunday evening my parents drove me to Sacramento and wished me luck as I boarded a plane to Seattle. I didn't know what I was doing but it didn't matter. I was getting away from things and on my way to someplace else and that was all that I cared about.

2

I got off the plane in Seattle and wondered what to do next. I knew I had to get on a plane to get to Anchorage but I wasn't sure when I was going to leave, either right away or after a day or two. I was going to call someone first. I knew that Yasu lived in Seattle now and there was a chance I could hang out with him in the city for a while, and maybe then I could get more info on the canneries in Alaska and where I could get a job there or what city would have the most opportunities. But I didn't have much money so staying in Seattle didn't seem like much of an option, but I figured I would try anyway. I found a pay phone and called his number. Someone other than him answered.

"Hello, may I speak to Yasu?" I said.

"He's not here right now," said the man. "He's out with some of his friends." I knew that this person must have been part of the couple with whom Yasu was living, the people he had told me about when he had come back to visit all of us.

"Do you know when he'll be back?"

"No, sorry. Would you like to leave a message?"

I thought about this. Frankly, I didn't like Yasu at all any more because of his recent behavior toward me back in Koreatown. I really didn't want to spend time with him. The only reason I had called was because I thought he might be willing to help me, but then I doubted that he could do that given how unfamiliar everything, including the canneries, was to him and how he hadn't been able to help me earlier.

"That's all right," I said. "Bye." I hung up. Even if Yasu had been able to help me, I don't think I would have liked his company. Too much had happened between us. So I sat down and looked around the airport. It was very quiet. I could see the nearby metropolitan area through the tall windows and it was very dark outside and I felt alone. It was time for me to go to Alaska. So I got up, grabbed my bags, and walked over to the Alaska Airlines counter and bought a one-way ticket to Anchorage. It was time to move on and after a few hours I was on a plane bound for the great unknown.

A long flight ensued and eventually we landed in Anchorage and it was the middle of the night. I slept on the floor of the airport with some other passengers. The next day I boarded a bus south to Kenai. Soon I got a job, a less difficult job than I had imagined it would be, and settled onto Kodiak Island and began to work in a cannery. After a few days I called Jose.

"I made it," I said. "I'm up in Alaska."

"Did you find work?" he asked.

"Yeah, at this great place, with free room and board and everything on this island far away. I sure wish you guys could come up."

"Me too."

I'm not sure why I had called him, except that maybe I missed the whole gang from L.A. and that I had been telling everyone about my plans to go to Alaska for over a month and I wondered if they thought I would do it or not. Maybe I wanted to prove that I had done it because in the back of my mind there had been a lot of disbelief.

We talked for a while about some little things but soon there was nothing more to be said. My life was different now and his was the same.

"I better go," I said. "Tell David I said hello."

"I will, bye." He hung up and that was the last time I ever spoke to him.

It didn't take me long to meet the other guys working at the cannery and soon I became comfortable enough to share some of my experiences.

"Where are you from?" asked one guy one day.

"Los Angeles," I answered.

"This must be a real change for you, up where there's hardly anybody."

"You're not kidding. No movie stars up here."

"Did you see a lot down there?"

"Oh yeah, but more the first time I lived there, when I worked at the movie magazine." I proceeded to tell them of the many movie and television stars I had seen or heard about during the six-month period in 1995 when I lived in Beverly Hills. "But the funny thing is that there's always a movie or TV show being filmed all over the city."

"What's that like?"

"Well, there was that one time when I was walking downtown and I stopped and look around and there were all these people who looked like aliens, like the ones from that show "Alien Nation.""

"I remember that."

"So I looked at them and wondered what they were doing and then I saw some cameras and lighting equipment and I realized that I was on their set, that they were filming or rehearsing outside of this big building."

"What did you do?"

"I just kept walking until I got away from everybody. Nobody said anything so luckily I hadn't interrupted a scene or rehearsal or anything like that."

"That's funny, I've never even see a film crew before."

"Oh, they're all over the place but eventually they get intrusive. I woke up one morning at my apartment building and went downstairs on my way to work and the whole lobby was jam-packed, densely packed, with all these movie people and actors and lights and equipment and cameras and they were filming these scenes near the elevator and the front desk and all I can remember was being upset because I had to walk all around them and fight to get outside so I could leave for work. Or that time when they were filming that movie "Volcano" with Tommy Lee Jones, and my friends and I were going to the Beverly Center, this big mall, and there were tons of trucks and cameras and all this fake ash all over the ground and these big signs about how they were filming at that moment and by being there we were giving implied permission that they could film us if they did so. That's another story because my good friend was an extra in that film and he met Tommy Lee Jones and all this other stuff."

"That's so exciting," said one of my new friends on this island in Kodiak, Alaska. "I sure wish I could see stuff like that."

"Just go on down there. You're virtually guaranteed to see a movie star or a film being made, even if you don't want to."

"Maybe I will."

This really helped me make friends in Alaska, this talking about celebrities and movies and film sets and the whole L.A. lifestyle. And slowly during my time in Alaska I started to receive lots of letters from Sakura and it was great to hear from her and she wrote first about how unhappy she was with me for leaving, but things got better as I wrote to her to try to explain some of my reasons for getting away and what I was doing in Alaska. I promised her over and over that we would be together again, that I hadn't left her, that I still loved her. And I always meant it meant every word I said.

3

June 9, 1997

Dear Darrin,

I got a postcard from you today, thank you!! Where are you now? Are you o.k.? Are you alive? Are you... You just disappeared from me. I am angry at you!... No, I am not. I just, I was expecting to see you. I was waiting for your call that day when we promised to meet each other. And... I called you, but the man told me that you left. I ran to the chancellor. but you have already left. I could not believe it. I could not... How could you do this to me. How? Were you expecting this since we met? You really enjoy this, don't you!?

You wanted to leave L.A. as soon as possible. Oh, now really. Tell me the truth. You hate me, don't you? Now I sleep with your picture every night. Do you know how much I miss you? you think I am stupid? You do!! and I am thinking that I was not good enough for you, was I?

I could not do anything after you left for three days. But I thought I should stand up by myself. I am not a baby. I can not stay at home all day.

I can walk. I should do something. I will have grown up before you come back. And I will be beautiful and smart.

Anyway, how did you get there? by boat? I don't know how to get there. and it is too far. too far from here! how is the weather? is it cold? do you need a sweater? what is Alaska like?

I hope you got my letter, and please write to me. I am looking forward to get a letter from you. I miss you. I really miss you and... I love you. That's really how I feel.

Love, Sakura

*The other letter that I wanted to give you before you left for Alaska is here.

4

Dear Darrin,

I did not know that you are leaving so soon. so… I don't know what to say. and what to do. Just I wanted to be told more earlier. I am still not ready. I can not believe it. I do not want you to leave. I can not believe that you are going far away. Are you trying hurt me again? What is that about? What do you think, how many times you made me cry? not just one time. ten times!

I miss you already. How can I make smile without you. How? I want to go to Malibu with you again, and Montana street. I have seen many movies with you since I met you. But this is not enough. I want to go many places with you. such as San Francisco, New York and Europe. I am not going to go anywhere. until you will come back here. never, ever. I can not leave. I will be here, and I will wait for you. Even if you go far away, I will not forget you. I decided that I will wait for you. Like you decided to go to Alaska.

You told me before that if you did not love a person, you couldn't say "I love you." But now I know… this is Love… so, can I say that?

I love you.

Do you believe me? It is the truth. I love Darrin Atkins.

I wish you will be satisfied with your new job and you will enjoy it with your friends. But also, I hope you will come back soon. I can wait because I love you. So, do not die until you come back, and do not take drugs too much. Take care of yourself. I wish you will make a lot of money!

Don't forget me.
Don't say "Bye"
Please say "see you soon"
Don't say "It's over"
Don't say "we are finished"
please say "You will come back soon"
please promise me "You will never hurt me. You will never make me cry."
I can meet you soon, can't I?!

I LOVE YOU

Sakura

5

"You sure get a lot of letters," said one of my friends at the salmon cannery on Kodiak Island in Alaska. "Who are they from?"

"My Japanese girlfriend."

"Is she in Japan?" he asked.

"No, still in L.A. I left her there so I could come up here."

"Tell me that again. You left a girl to work at a cannery up here?"

"Well, there were other reasons. I wanted to stay but I hated my boring job and my car needed repairs and I just felt that it was time to go."

"At least you get some letters."

"She's very good about writing, maybe too good."

"Would you read us some of it?"

"Sure. Let me get one that's kinda mushy." I found the best one of the bunch, a letter that Sakura had written to me about how much she missed me, and I read that one to them.

"You better keep her," said my friend. "She obviously means it."

"I'm gonna try. I just don't know what's going to happen next."

My friend left and I stayed in my room and thought about Sakura. I was very far from her now, too far in many ways, and I wondered if I could ever get back to her. I just didn't know. I wrote her a long letter then and told her that I missed her a lot too and that I desperately wanted to see her again, and I promised her that we would definitely see each other again if she would just wait for me. Just wait for me is all that I asked and that was probably too much to ask of her.

The work during the summer at the cannery was cut short because of a fish shortage and a resulting strike. When I got back to California from Alaska, I didn't stay long in Stockton. I moved right away to Arizona to live on a ranch in Winslow. The first thing I did when I got my address there was write to Sakura and let her know where she could write to me and where I was living and what I was doing. I knew that we still had a chance of being together. I still cared for her a lot and desperately wanted to see her again. She was still in L.A. and I figured there was half a chance I could travel there or she could meet me somewhere in Arizona.

I worked on a ranch with some relatives and we built fences and did all the other things you could imagine one could do on a ranch. My heart was with Sakura and I thought of here when I was out alone on the barren land, when I put in hundreds of t-poles for barbed wire fences, when the days and the work seemed to stretch into infinity. She was with me when I was out there and her kind letters helped me survive many lonely nights in the small shed in which I slept. I dreamed of seeing her again and being in her arms. I wondered if there was even a remote chance of us getting together one last time. I kept that hope alive because it was all that I had, all that I had on that ranch in the middle of nowhere.

6

Aug. 20, 1997

Dear Darrin,

Hi Darrin! I thought you are in your home with your parents. But you are in Arizona!? What a surprise!

How are you doing? Are you o.k.? I really miss you! Are you fine? Thank you for writing to me and telling me where you are now!! and sending me your picture from Alaska. I like it. It's on the wall in my room, you're smiling!! and I got your letter today. I'm so happy with that!! I've been really missing you! so much. And I really want to see you as soon as possible. so, let's meet!!

I still want to see you because I like you, because you are the only one that I can tell anything. So please call me, soon!!

take care, don't drink too much!!

I love you!!

Sakura

7

Soon I grew tired of the ranch lifestyle so I packed up my stuff and drove to the nearest city which was Flagstaff, a place about ninety miles west of Winslow. I had grown weary of life on the ranch, mostly because it was so lonely out there and my thoughts always drifted to Sakura and how much I missed her and how I wanted to be with her again. It was during this time that I began to live in a campground in Flagstaff. I stayed here for a while and worked at some temporary jobs and ate sparingly.

Soon I applied via mail for a job at the Grand Canyon but the position wasn't scheduled to begin until October the first so I had some spare time before then. I worked at a couple jobs and saved money by living in a tent in the Fort Tuthill County Campground.

I wrote to Sakura a lot and knew that I wanted to go and visit her in Japan, which was where she had moved back. I made up my mind that I would definitely go. I didn't know how I would ever afford the trip or when it could happen but I was so confident in it coming to pass that I went to downtown Flagstaff and renewed my passport through the courthouse there. Believe me, I had very little money at this time, barely enough to survive, and no credit on my credit cards, but still I believed that I could make it all the way to Japan once I started work at the Grand Canyon and started saving money.

I stopped by the big used bookstore in Flagstaff and browsed through the magazines and books there. My first priority was getting a travel book on Japan and I found an inexpensive useful one. I wanted to send something to Sakura so I found two issues of Premiere magazine that were perfect. One was an issue from two years earlier with my name listed inside as an editorial intern. The other was a recent issue with Brad Pitt on the cover. I went to the post office, paid for a large envelope and the appropriate postage, and sent the magazines along to Sakura. I sent a letter to her separately because I knew it would get to her faster than the magazines and I wanted her to receive something from me in the next few days.

I left the campground on the morning of the first day of October and headed for the Grand Canyon where my future awaited me. I would be living in a dormitory with the other employees and would work at a hotel called the El Tovar at the south rim. I wondered what my life would be like and I hoped for the best. And still I thought of Sakura and couldn't wait to be with her again.

8

Oct. 8, 1997

Dear Darrin,

Hi, I got the letter from you! Thank you!! How are you doing today? I'm so happy that you wrote me back. and I was relieved that you are still alive and you're o.k. How do you like your new place? Have you made a new friend yet?

I've never been to Grand Canyon. Do you enjoy being there? I hope you are having fun! Do you cook your own meal by yourself? Please take care of your health.

You would like to come to Japan?! I'm so glad that you say so!! I'm so happy! Of course, you can visit me. No, I have to say "Please visit me" and see me, meet me!! Oh god I really miss you. I can't wait to meet you again!! I wish I could go there now and knock the door and say "hello" to you. I have every letter you wrote to me. Some of them are hanging on the wall in my room.

I'll write to you soon.

Love, Sakura

9

Oct. 27, 1997

Dear Darrin!

Hi, how are you doing? I got your letter and pages from the magazine today!! Thank you! Your name is on it! Do you want to go back and work at Premiere again?

How's dormitory life? Is it like Chancellor Hotel? And how's your roommate? Has he come back? I won't share a room with friend. It's difficult for me. I can stay friend's house sometimes. so... sometimes is good!

I met Rumi on October 18. She visited her old friend in Yokohama, so I could reach her. We went to Hard Rock Cafe and had dinner. and we talked many things. She was really fine and works at office as a telephone operator. She hasn't changed at all except her hair color. I had a good time!!

How was Halloween? It's finished, isn't it?! Did you have good time? I couldn't send a card... I'm sorry for that. I remember last Halloween. I didn't go to party.

I'll write you soon!! Take care! I miss you so much.

Love, Sakura

10

As I lived at the Grand Canyon, I started to prepare for my trip to Japan, although I still had no idea if or when I would go. I had already received my renewed passport from the government agency. I had to decide when to travel and this was the hard part because I figured it might be difficult to get enough time off from work. Plus, I wanted to make sure I went when Sakura had time off from her job. Lastly, I still had to come up with money, and a lot of it. The round-trip ticket would cost me over six hundred dollars to be sure. I had very little money in the bank and virtually no credit.

After my parents left for home after visiting me at the canyon, I sat down and looked at all the money I might be making in the coming months. Then I figured out when I wanted to visit her. Of course I wanted to go immediately but that wasn't going to happen. So I tried to figure out when was the soonest I could leave. I looked up the days when I got paid and how much I expected from those checks. And I thought about when I would need to buy the ticket. Finally, I came to the conclusion that I wanted to visit her over Valentine's Day weekend around the middle of February, that I would probably receive enough money by then, and that the only thing would be for me to get that time off from work.

Of course there were other things to consider. I would need to save every penny I could find and I wouldn't have much money for food or other things during my life at the Grand Canyon. I would have to go down to Phoenix to purchase the ticket and that was a consideration because my car no longer worked and had been abandoned by me in the parking lot. But Valentine's Day weekend was perfect because of its inherent romanticism, because it occurred at the perfect time around my pay periods, because I would get a check right before I would depart from Japan, and for lots of other reasons. I would do everything I could to make sure it worked out for us this way, that I could fly to Japan to be with Sakura on Valentine's Day for one of the best vacations imaginable.

The first thing was to call Sakura to make sure she wanted me to come visit her. Although she had said yes in one of her letters back in October, I wanted to check again to make sure. It was, after all, a big thing for me, that of flying to Japan by myself to be with her. Two days before Christmas I found a pay phone, dialed my phone card number and then her number, and waited nervously to speak to Sakura. I had learned a few simple phrases to use in case someone other than Sakura answered the phone.

"Hello?" I said when someone finally answered. "Hello?" I could tell immediately that it was not Sakura so I quickly tried some of my Japanese phrases. Luckily, at that moment, a small group of young Japanese tourists came into the lodge. I said some more words in Japanese on the phone and the tourists looked at me in surprise. Then I motioned to one of them and she came over to me.

"I'm trying to call my girlfriend in Japan," I said. "I think her mother answered. Would you help me?"

This girl was kind enough to get on the phone and speak in Japanese to whomever was on the other end of the line. The girl stopped, asked me my name and who I was trying to reach, and I told her. After a minute she looked at me.

"She's not home right now," she said.

"Okay, would you tell them that Darrin tried to call Sakura and that I will call again in a few days?"

She did this and then said goodbye and hung up. I thanked her a lot and then went back to my room. It was frustrating not to be able to call Sakura and speak to her directly.

On Christmas Day, I got up really early and found a pay phone at Maswik Lodge. Surely she had to be home on this day. The phone rang and rang and then someone answered and it was her and I was greatly relieved. We had a wonderful conversation and it was great to hear her voice.

"I want to come visit you on Valentine's Day weekend," I said. "I can buy my ticket next month if you want me to come."

Sakura said that she wanted that and would be excited about it and would plan many things for us. We talked on and on about it and then I mentioned that my phone card was running out of time and I had to go.

"Merry Christmas," I said.

"You too, Merry Christmas. I love you."

"I love you too. Bye."

I hung up and walked back to my cabin at the Grand Canyon to open some gifts that my parents had left for me during their visit. I felt a lot better knowing that I was going to fly to Japan in February and that I would see Sakura one last time. And I dreamed and dreamed some more of what it would be like there and how wonderful our time together would be and how grand the weekend most definitely could be, and I knew that the next eight weeks would seem like forever. And of course they did.

II

Dec. 25, 1997

Dear Darrin,

How are you doing? It's me again. and thank you for calling me on Christmas!! I just got a call from you ten minutes ago. I'm so happy and very, very thank you. Gosh, I'm so excited!! Do you understand how I feel? I haven't heard your voice for 6 months. You are so nice!!

And also I'm sorry that when you tried calling me, my grandfather answered it, but he can't speak English. And I wasn't told until next day. On 24th in the evening, my grandmother told me she had a call from an American and Japanese girl. Even my parents knew that. then I asked them if they knew about that. They said, "Oh yes... we just forget telling you." I couldn't believe it! I was really furious at them. But I am really happy now!!

By the way. Please come to Japan and visit me! I do want to see you!! So much I miss you! When can you come? I'll show you around! Whenever is fine to me! So let's make a plan on something!

I'll write a letter again! Take care and don't catch a cold!! Good night!!

I love you.

Love, Sakura

Jan. 5, 1998

Dear Darrin,

Hi, how are you today? I got the post card from you today! It's beautiful and thank you so much. And what a wonderful idea, on Valentine's
Day?! I would really like to spend with you, too!! Of course, yes! It's okay
with me very much!! I can't wait until then! How long will you stay? Just
for 4 days? well, it's okay, I can spend with you. I'm so happy and excited!!

Is there something you want to see or visit or eat in Japan? If you have
any interest about Japan, tell me that!! I'll go to the library to check up this
weekend! I want to go many places with you. Take care and see you...
soon! I miss you so much!!

Love, Sakura

p.s. tell me when you will arrive in Japan. I'll be there.

Jan. 17, 1998

Dear Darrin,

How are you? Thank you for calling me last night (Jan. 16). We couldn't talk much, but it was good to talk to you again! And I received your letter of Jan. 8 today. I was so surprised that it was written five sentences in Japanese.! It was great!! It was hard to write and speak Japanese, wasn't it? But you wrote them very well! It was very nice. I was deeply moved!! Thank you so much.

AND You bought the ticket! I can't wait either!! When you arrive at the airport, I will be waiting for you! (Narita airport) It's been snowing and raining these days. It's so cold! I wish the weather will be good when we spend together.

Valentine's Day is coming up soon.

That sounds nice that you live in a cabin! and you can see lots of deer. You live in beautiful surroundings. It's very different from Los Angeles, isn't it? And you cook yourself? Or is there someone cook for you? If I were there, I could cook for you. And it's good to hear that you are doing well!!

I'm really looking forward to meeting you! I'll write to you again. Take care and see you!! Have a good sleep and sweet dreams,

Love, Sakura

12

And then it was February the twelfth. I left the Grand Canyon on a bus and it took me south to Phoenix where I got on the plane and was soon on my way to Japan. My next stop was L.A. where I would transfer to a Korean plane headed for Japan. I was nervous as I made the short flight over to Los Angeles from Phoenix. I wondered if I was doing the right thing, wondered if Sakura would find me at the Tokyo airport, wondered if things would be better than when I flew to Germany as a teenager and got lost inside the airport for over an hour.

I got to the L.A. airport and everything was familiar to me again, the terminals, the cab drivers, the taxis, the recordings on the loudspeakers, the design of the airport, the luggage retrieval areas, the employee uniforms, the buses outside, and everything else. I actually missed that job I had as a skycap, but not that much.

I made my way outside and onto the sidewalk on the lower level and followed it up two terminals to the international terminal. I was nervous and excited. I checked the departure times and found out that I was right on schedule. I stopped in a gift shop and bought a newspaper and a couple magazines. My flight was scheduled to last ten and a half hours and I knew I would need something to read.

Finally, I went and checked in at the Korean Airlines counter and then went through security and then to my terminal where I waited for an hour. It was strange to see the message near my gate, how I was departing from Los Angeles and my destination was Tokyo. Before I knew it I was on the plane and it was taking off for Japan and I didn't know how I had gotten that far and I recalled the time a few months earlier when I had been living in that campsite and how certain I was that I would be going to Japan to see Sakura in the early part of the next year and here it was finally happening. And I couldn't believe it, couldn't believe it at all. And oh how I missed Sakura.

And finally I got to Japan and took my time and wasn't in a hurry and grabbed my bag and walked out of the plane and into the Tokyo airport terminal. I followed the signs and arrows and made it to a booth, with someone who spoke English, where I was instructed to fill out a form that indicated where and with whom I would be staying during my visit. I filled it out and then walked around and tried to find Sakura but she wasn't anywhere. I waited and looked all over and she was nowhere to be found and after forty minutes of looking I realized that maybe she hadn't shown up and I didn't blame her at all because of how I had treated her back in L.A. and after that. I deserved this. I deserved to be abandoned at the airport in a foreign country and I knew this and wasn't angry at all because I had been awfully mean to Sakura on too many occasions and never for a good reason. I was getting what I deserved.

I realized that I couldn't sleep in the airport and I knew that I had to find a hotel for the night. So I had my bags checked at the exit, converted some American currency into Japanese yen, and then I decided to leave. I opened the door and there was a whole bunch of people waiting in this giant room outside. I quickly scanned the faces and to my great relief I noticed Sakura and quickly raced over to her and hugged her tight and nearly cried with joy and relief.

"Did you have to wait long?" I asked.

"Oh, yes."

"I'm so sorry. I was looking for you inside all this time. Thanks so much for waiting."

"It's okay, let's go to the train."

We were together again and I was filled with happiness and satisfaction and I could tell that she was too and it was a miracle that we were together again and I couldn't believe it, not even for one damn second.

13

It was a nice day in Japan as we took the train east from the Tokyo airport to the city of Yokohama. I felt a hell of a lot better just being by her side. I had been more than a little scared at the prospect of not being able to be with her in Japan and being alone in a foreign country without any help, and I think I learned a big lesson from it.

"We can go to the apartment first," she said to me. "So you can drop off your bags. Is this all you have?" she asked, pointing to my backpack.

"Yes. I didn't want to bring too much, partly because I didn't want to lose anything."

"Oh. I told my parents you were coming."

"Is it okay?"

"Oh, yes. They know I like you, that you're from America."

"Where will I sleep?"

"In my room."

"Okay, fine by me." Actually, I couldn't wait to sleep and that was the only thing on my mind. It was just after noon that day and already I was exhausted. The time change and my inability to sleep on the plane were catching up to me. The train ride lasted a little less than an hour. Then we took the subway for a while.

"How far to your place?" I asked.

"We're almost there, just a little more."

We got off at a subway stop and made our way out of the subway system. Once up at ground level we walked for a while and then boarded a bus.

"I've missed you a lot," I said.

"Me too, I've missed you."

Soon, after the bus drove for about six blocks, we got off and walked a few blocks.

"There it is, up there at the corner," she said.

By this time I was completely burnt out and I desperately needed to stop for a while. At the entrance Sakura and I took off our shoes and walked into a very small apartment, at least from my perspective. A woman came from the left and greeted me. I said hello in Japanese and Sakura told me it was her mother. Sakura told her what our plans were for the rest of the day. Then we went upstairs to her room. On the way I observed that the doorways and doors were nearly a foot shorter than those in America and the tip of my head nearly hit the top of the doorway. We walked into her room and I sat down on her bed and I was more tired than I could believe it.

"I love your body," I said and when she turned around I smiled because of the double meaning of the phrase. Then I pointed to her body figure in the room which she used for her fashion work and clothing designs and styles.

"Oh, funny."

"I've got this chance at a teaching job and maybe I can do it in New York," I said. "And you can join me and do fashion there."

"I'd like that."

"Me too. We could find an apartment together. We wouldn't need a car at all, just the subway to get us around."

"Yes, I hope you get it."

"You could really develop your fashion career there," I said.

I saw an issue of Premiere magazine on her wall that I had sent to her when I was in Arizona, the issue with Brad Pitt on the cover. This issue was the one I had sent with a letter, the one where Sakura had written back to me and asked if I was thinking about going back to Premiere to work.

"My mother asked me if that was you."

"I wish it was," I said. I figured Sakura hadn't fully explained to her mother that I had worked at the magazine and only for a brief period a few years earlier, or that I wasn't an actor or model.

"You still have the Disney figurine," I said when I saw it on a bookshelf in her room.

"Yes. I should have crushed it." She smiled at this and had been only half joking. I still loved her wit and biting sarcasm because it meant that she had personality.

"I know. I'm sorry I was mean to you. Really, I am very sorry."

"It's okay."

That night we went to a Mexican restaurant. Then to a small cafe but I was too tired to do anything more than that. I wanted to stay awake most of the time I was with her but that could not be done. Jet lag was getting to me and I was completely worn out. We were back in her room by ten o'clock that night. I wanted to stay awake as much as I could but I knew I wouldn't enjoy my time if I did that. Eventually I fell asleep on her bed while she watched a Christian Slater movie about plants and romance, and I was grateful that she let me sleep in her big, comfortable bed and that she was kind enough to sleep on the floor. Oh, how happy I was that I was in Japan and back in the company of my love.

14

All her relatives and family members were there to meet me in the kitchen downstairs on Saturday morning and it was intimidating because I didn't know the language and it was hard to communicate with them. But they were all very nice and friendly and seemed eager to meet and know the American. I tried to speak as much Japanese as I could, but most of the time Sakura worked as the translator. I met her aunt and uncle and their young twin girls and all of them lived in the apartment complex above from Sakura's. I met her mother and father and grandmother and they seemed nice and kind.

After I met everyone and we finished breakfast, I called my parents. I hadn't told anybody in my family that I was going to Japan because I didn't want them to worry about me and half of me hadn't believed that I would even make it.

"Hello," I said when my mother answered. I didn't let on where I was calling from and pretended that I was still at the Grand Canyon and that nothing was out of the ordinary. Finally I said something. "I'm in Japan right now, in Yokohama, visiting my girlfriend from L.A.."

"No, you're not."

"I am, seriously. This is the surprise I had told you about before."

And of course my mother was amazed and told me to do lots of things and have a great time and I promised I would send postcards home, and then I hung up quickly because it was long distance.

After eleven o'clock Sakura and I set out on our first full day in Japan and I was excited and told her that I wanted to go to some shops and places that lots of others went to. So we hopped on a bus and then made it to the subway and started along. On the way I saw some people who wore white surgical masks over their mouths.

"Are they doctors and nurses?" I asked.

"No, they're sick," she said. "We do that so other people stay away from them and don't get their germs."

"That's great. I wish we had something like that."

"It lets people know to stay away."

Then we got to an intersection in the street.

"Are these flowers free?" I said as I pointed down to the curb where there was a nice container filled with pretty flowers. "We could take them to your place."

"No," she said as she laughed. "Someone died there. We can't take them."

I had figured that that was what they were there for. "Wow, we have that in the U.S. too."

And for most of the day we went around to different shops and outside market places and I took lots of pictures and it was a lovely time. We went to the Nakamisc shopping mall which led to famous Sensouji Buddhist temple, and we took lots of pictures of each other. Sakura showed me around and explained everything to me about the temple and its significance. And we rode the subway to other places and saw more things and took more pictures.

We went to Tokyo that night and I marveled at all the neon lights and it was the best place I had ever been, better than New York in my mind, and I loved it because of all the lights and excitement and people and culture. We stopped at a place called Condomania and of course we loved it there because there were condoms for sale, condoms of every shape, color, size, and texture.

"We should buy a lot of condoms," I said. "In case we need to use them."

"You promise to use them all?"

"Of course." I knew there was a reason why I liked Sakura so much.

Then we went to a small Japanese restaurant across the street from a sushi restaurant, which we didn't go to because it was really expensive, according to Sakura, and there was a long line of people out front. This small restaurant we went to was cool and fun and quaint and colorful and we were taken to a small booth in the back and on the left. I liked it immediately.

"What kind of food do you like?" asked Sakura.

"Hamburgers, mostly," I joked. I was just kidding and Sakura knew it because she often said that the only American food was hamburgers. "No, I like spicy food."

"Spicy like me?"

"Exactly."

"Okay." Sakura looked at her menu while I got out my camera. Then I turned it toward her and was going to take her picture but she kept putting up her hand.

"Just one picture," I said.

"No, I don't like pictures."

Just then she had to sneeze so I took a picture of her while her hands were down.

After we ordered and when the food came, Sakura took the camera and took a few photos of me. One, which I still have, is of me eating the soup and noodles with my chopsticks. There's an employee in an orange shirt and white cap standing behind me at the counter. And right after she took it I felt a splash from my soup and somehow the liquid got into my eye and it burned terribly because it was so spicy. I tried to splash a little water into my eye from my glass but it wasn't enough.

"Where are the bathrooms?" I asked her.

"Right behind you, back here."

I stumbled over to them and luckily nobody was inside. I leaned my head under the faucet and turned on the water and let it come right into my eye. After a minute of this I started to feel better and then went back to the table.

"I'm all right now," I said.

"Is it spicy enough?"

"Yes, enough indeed."

After dinner we walked around the neighborhood for a while and then we went to a small French cafe a few blocks away. It was really nice and had a very French ambiance and we didn't mind waiting for a table and then when we were seated we just ordered some pastries and hot drinks and enjoyed them at our table and enjoyed each other's company and everything was wonderful and memorable.

15

And then the next day was Valentine's Day and we spent the early part of the day taking the subway to Tokyo from Yokohama. There we did some more shopping and I found some bags of Japanese candy that I wanted to send home to my relatives and of course I bought some postcards too. We stopped at a post office later to get some stamps from a vending machine. Sakura put some money in and then selected some stamps. When she got her change, she seemed surprise.

"What's wrong?" I asked.

"Someone forgot their change," she said. "It's a lot of money."

"That's a good omen. Let's go."

Then we went to the fish market, which was something that I wanted to do, but the fish had already been sold. On the walk back to the subway I bought a soda in a vending machine but it turned out to be hot tea in a can and I couldn't believe it. I wanted something cold because it was a bit humid and overcast.

In the late afternoon we went out for dinner to a very nice Italian restaurant, and it was a wonderful meal and we had most of the place to ourselves. After dinner we went across the street to Tokyo Tower and by now it was fully lit and very bright and awfully romantic and I couldn't believe how beautiful it looked and how wonderful it was that I was with Sakura again and that we were together on Valentine's Day in Tokyo. We went inside the entrance and then took the elevators up to the viewing area. Then we found a wonderful spot and held hands and looked out over Tokyo and it was unbelievable and romantic and special and every other wonderful word that can be uttered and I was happy, very happy indeed.

We stayed out late and enjoyed the lights of the city and made the best use of our time together that we could. And then, back at her place, we fooled around in her room in the dark before we went to sleep. And I guess I was making too much noise though I tried hard not to. Her mom knocked on the door and said something in Japanese and I quickly rolled myself off her bed and onto the blankets on the floor. Sakura talked back to her mother and said something and then they exchanged unpleasant words and I realized that I had put everyone in an awkward position. Finally the mother went away.

"Come back," said Sakura to me.

I joined her again on the bed. "Maybe we shouldn't do this."

"It's okay, it's normal."

Still, I didn't want things to become worse between Sakura and her parents. I dreaded having to look at her family in the morning. The good thing was that I was leaving the next day. Besides, I knew the culture and knew that everyone would be polite and considerate and nobody would make an embarrassing scene. I slept well this night and was content at all the things we had done that day and it was the best day ever.

16

On Sunday we did a lot of fun things. We went to the big aquarium nearby after a ride there by Sakura's uncle, the firefighter, and after the show Sakura bought some souvenirs for her small female cousins.

"You're getting the same thing for both of them?" I asked her.

"I have to. If not, they'll argue."

And I thought this was interesting, how it was so similar to every other family on the planet and I didn't know why I thought things would be different for Japanese families. I didn't want to sleep on Sunday night because I knew I would be leaving the next morning.

We woke on Monday and I could feel that the end of my visit with Sakura was over, and I hated that fact.

"What about your job?" I asked her.

"Oh yes, I nearly forgot." She smiled at this and I thought it was funny. I watched her find the number and then speak in Japanese on the phone for a few minutes. Then she hung up.

"What did you say?" I asked her.

"Just that I was sick."

"You're not going to get into trouble?"

"No, no."

"Make sure you wear one of those paper masks over your mouth so they'll think you were really sick."

"I will," she said.

We got dressed and then made our way downstairs. After breakfast, I gathered all my things and we headed to the subway station. We got there and then she remembered something and had to have her mother bring her passport. We got that and then took the train for a while until we were at a mall. There we bought some postcards and I got one for free. And for the first time, at the foot of the escalator, a mall employee bowed to us as we entered the store and I thought it was the coolest thing ever, because I had never been bowed to before.

Then we had trouble with the train and the tickets but finally we made it to the airport. Once there I had her buy me a Fiji apple because they looked so delicious and I just had to have one, and I noticed how the change from the transaction was placed on a small tray and the tray handed to Sakura for her to remove the money. And I knew that this was an additional way of keeping things sanitary, of reducing the passage of germs, much like the wearing of white masks by those who are sick. Then I couldn't believe that there was an airport exit fee because I was out of money completely.

"Do you have any money for this?" I asked her and it was a miracle that she did and that she gave it to me. It came to about twenty dollars in U.S. currency and it only served to remind me that I would be terribly poor when I got back to the Grand Canyon. I felt lucky to already have my return plane and bus tickets to get me back to my cabin because I certainly didn't have any money or credit to purchase them.

And we hugged long and close and I had to go and so I walked down the escalator and followed the signs to my terminal. She kept following me from above and kept waving to me and I waved back until we lost sight of each other for good, and I didn't want to leave at all.

Soon I was on a plane and headed back to the states and the whole experience got to me and I started to cry and I couldn't help it one bit because I knew deep down that I would never see Sakura again and that hurt me to the bone. There was too much of a distance between us, an entire ocean in fact, and too much of a language and cultural barrier. Sure, I still hoped that we would get together and in the months to come I would try to get a teaching job so she could come to America and we could live together and be happy. But this wouldn't pan out and she would eventually go on with her life and I would go on with mine and losing her would hurt me quite a lot and I would never get over it.

17

Feb. 17, 1998

Dear Darrin

How are you? How was the plane when you got back to home? and an apple? I almost broke into tears when I got back to the station alone... I forgot to say "Thank you for coming here, spending a great time with me, holding me deeply, and eating the chocolate which I made." But your love is better than chocolate! I had a really great time. It was just like a dream. Holding your arm, walking on a street, you were just in front of me, smiling to me, talking to me, it was great time! You were with me!! I really enjoyed! I didn't want to wake up this morning because I still wanted to dream in my bed... Well... One of my dreams has come true. You know what? I met you and spent together again.

I've been thinking about you since you left here. I can't wait to meet you again. When I wait a train, when I walk down the street, there is only you in my mind. All my think is just about you. I can't stop thinking about you.

I went to work today. and wore a mask on my mouth. and they believed that I was sick. It worked out!!

I really want to go there to see you. How long should I wait? I don't think I can wait until summer. It's hard to wait every day. A day and even one minute seems long to me. I love you SO much. You are the only one. I miss you so much. I'll write to you soon.

xxx ooo

Love, Sakura

18

Sakura and I wrote many letters to each other after my trip to Japan. Unfortunately, things just didn't work out between us and a lot had to do with the fact that there was a huge ocean that separated us and that whole thing about long-distance relationships is awfully true. It's too hard to keep in touch and keep things going between two people who are so very far away from each other.

Three weeks after I came back from Japan I took a bus from the Grand Canyon to Los Angeles for an interview for a job as a teacher in a special recruitment program for urban cities and rural towns with teacher shortages. The bus arrived early in the morning in L.A. in the downtown area and I walked the two miles to the subway terminal. While there I couldn't help but think back to all the times when I had ridden the subway when I had lived in Koreatown, the times when I had gone to the L.A. city library with Sakura, and the times when I had made some of Harry's movies downtown, in particular "Over the Edge." I remembered when I sat outside one of the subway entrances and Harry had taken a picture of me sitting on my briefcase, during a rest from our filming. As I walked down the steps to the subway and train stations, I thought back to all my time in Koreatown and L.A. and how it was all long gone now and it had gone way too fast, so fast that I could hardly believe any of it had happened at all.

I took the light rail train south and then all the way west to El Segundo. I had to walk after the train stopped but it didn't take too long to get to the building where my interview would be, and the place happened to be located right across the street from the Wolfgang Puck Cafe where I had worked before, and I wondered what the chances of that were, of my potential future being fifty feet away from my distant past. And I thought of how this job I wanted was a chance for a future for Sakura and me and here it was so close to our past life together.

In the interview I met with some of the people and they asked me where I wanted to work and what other restrictions I had. I was quite specific in mentioning that I wanted to work in New York City and that I had a girlfriend with whom I wanted to live.

"Are you two married?" she asked.

"No, not yet."

"Engaged?"

"No," I said. "Actually, she's in Japan now, but if I get this job then she will come and live with me."

"Well, unless you're married, it would be difficult for us to make living arrangements for both of you. You might have a better chance with the rural areas."

"No, it has to be urban and in a big city. New York if possible."

"Okay, we'll see what we can do." Then she asked me a lot of other questions and then I had an interview with someone else.

After the morning session of the interview, I went to the Wolfgang Puck cafe for lunch and it was weird being there again after being gone for two years, and I was amazed that there was one employee, who happened to serve me lunch, that I recognized and who had been there with me and worked with me when the place first opened so long ago. So then I went back to the interview and I was supposed to give a sample lesson plan and of course mine was on the geography and culture of Japan.

"Have you ever been there?" someone asked after I had gotten started.

"I just got back last month," I said.

"Did you go for the Olympics?"

"No, actually I went for Valentine's weekend to be with my girlfriend. I stayed four days."

"Seems like kind of a waste," added someone else. "All those miles for such a short time."

"Both of us had jobs and we couldn't get off for too long. And I really wanted to be with her again so that's all that mattered to me."

I continued with my lesson and it went quite well and soon it was all over and I made my way back to the light rail station and then all the way back downtown to the bus station. I got on the next bus and the next day I was back at my cabin at the Grand Canyon.

Two weeks later I found out that I didn't get the job as a teacher like I had hoped and our dream of living together in New York City, with me as a teacher and Sakura as a fashion designer, never came to fruition. I'm sure that the lack of a job offer had a lot to do with the fact that I specified that I wanted to live with Sakura, that I wanted us to be in New York City and no other place, and that I wouldn't even consider other possibilities. But this was what Sakura and I wanted and I didn't want to settle for anything else.

This was a great disappointment to me because I thought that I had a good chance at the position and I didn't get it and didn't understand why. The worst part was that I had built it up, that I had had Sakura tell her family that I was going to be a teacher, that I gave her the impression that it was going to happen, and now it simply wasn't going to happen at all. It was depressing and I didn't want to believe it. After all this mess, things started to go downhill for me. The teaching position had been our last hope of getting together again, of her moving to the U.S. permanently. There wasn't much I could do after this and it didn't take long for our letters to each other to stop altogether.

19

I have lost touch with everyone. The last I heard about Shizu was that she was back in Japan and maybe she went back to her fiancee and maybe she didn't and I really don't give a damn either way. I think Sakura told me that Shizu was getting married finally and that just killed me, the fact that she had been engaged to some guy during all the time she had been in L.A. and had been with Harry in the Biblical sense and now she was going to be married like nothing had happened and like she had been absolutely faithful. Maybe it's not so funny after all.

I got a letter from Harry that year and then one a little bit after that. I stopped writing to him at one point because of what he was doing to my story "Dark City Nights" and how he was tearing it apart with his revisions until nothing was left of my original concept. This shouldn't have surprised me at all given my experiences at Premiere and my knowledge of the development of movies and how so many people get involved and how a story can change dramatically because of the demands of everyone else. I guess I should be grateful that we finished the short movies "Trouble on the Home Front" and "Over the Edge." And that we came close to finishing "Dirty Laundry."

Harry informed me that David and Jose had each moved back to Spain at different times and then later that they moved back to L.A. together and ended up in the same apartment complex as Harry.

The only person that I'm still friends with is Rebecca and I try hard to write to her and keep in touch as often as I can. This isn't easy given how often she moves around Europe. Last year she was living in France, then she was in Spain for a while, but now I think she's back in Sweden. I sure hope she continues her photography studies because she's awfully good at it. I'm planning on flying to Stockholm to visit her next year and let's hope it happens because I want to remain friends with at least one person from that great time in my life. And if Stockholm doesn't happen, well, I'm definitely going to London soon and maybe we can meet up there.

And I guess I'm tired of Hollywood and movies and the whole entertainment industry. Sure, it's fun and all and I always buy the new issues of Premiere and examine each page because I can't help myself. And I will always keep that trunk full of a hundred old issues of Premiere, ones that go back a long time ago. I still have all my old Super 8 movie equipment, the cameras and lights and viewfinders and projectors, but I think I might get rid of all that soon. Everything's digital these days and people can make movies on their computers with little effort at all and nobody needs anybody else. They can be their own writers, directors, producers and actors and they don't have to deal with anyone else if they don't want to, but where's the fun in that.

I miss the life in L.A. I'd much rather be back in Koreatown with Harry and Rebecca and Jose and David and Shizu. And I'd love to hang out with Sakura and go to the movies for free and go to the beaches late at night and do all kinds of other things. Damnit I would. I'd much rather be living at that hotel again and making student films and thinking about storyboards and lighting and slow-motion and action scenes and romance scenarios and brutal fight sequences between me and Jose. And I sure wish I was back at Premiere magazine because that was a whole heck of a lot of fun, that internship I had there in '95. I sure hate it when things have to change and I can't for the life of me figure out why I ever left L.A. Things were great then but now they're not so great and all I have left of that time in my life is a bunch of pictures and postcards and some memories that keep me up at night. I've got nothing, nothing much at all.

Sure, you can leave Hollywood and fly away to Alaska, but Hollywood never leaves you. It's a state of mind. I'm still in Hollywood though I live far away, though I reside in boring old Stockton. But I'm getting out real soon and getting back into the limelight and just you wait and see what happens to me next.

20

And maybe you're wondering what made me think about this whole story, what made me finally force myself to sit down and write about it. Well, I'm moving back down to L.A. very soon, next week actually, because I've missed the damn city too much and I've gotten a little homesick for the life down there. It's the end of May and I signed up with a casting agency in Burbank and they've got plenty of work and I'm moving out of Stockton and heading south. I plan on living in some campgrounds and taking it easy for a while, just relaxing and enjoying the beaches and having a grand old time. And of course I'll work on movies and television shows and be an extra on them and maybe even get a small cameo here and there, that would certainly be nice but if it doesn't happen that's okay too.

Sure, there's a girl in my life now, an Asian girl that I'm going to leave here in Stockton when I move back to the city of angels. I bet she's a big reason why I finished this book, because she reminds me so very much of Sakura, and every time I talk to her and every time I see her face and look into her eyes, I think back to Sakura and remember how I lost her forever. Yeah, I think back to how I lost her and how it was my own damn fault. I think back to how I could have kept her in my life and how we could have had many more glorious times together. I think back and realize that all those wonderful times with her are gone forever. And that just really tears me apart and this book is the only way I can keep her as a part of my life.

Oh Sakura, won't you give me one more chance? I wish things had ended up differently for us, I really wish they had, so always remember that I care for you and that I hope to see you again some day. And that day cannot come soon enough.

www.ingramcontent.com/pod-product-compliance
Lightning Source LLC
Chambersburg PA
CBHW061358280526
45784CB00001B/299